Desire for God and the Things of God

Desire for God
and the Things of God

The Relationships between
Christian Spirituality and Morality

Wyndy Corbin Reuschling

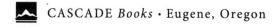

CASCADE *Books* • Eugene, Oregon

DESIRE FOR GOD AND THE THINGS OF GOD
The Relationships between Christian Spirituality and Morality

Cascade Books
An Imprint of Wipf and Stock Publishers
199 W. 8th Ave., Suite 3
Eugene, OR 97401

www.wipfandstock.com

ISBN 13: 978-1-60899-865-4

Cataloging-in-Publication data:

Reuschling, Wendy Corbin.

    Desire for God and the things of God : the relationships between Christian spirituality and morality / Wyndy Corbin Reuschling.

    xx + 134 p. ; 23 cm. —Includes bibliographical references and index.

    ISBN 13: 978-1-60899-865-4

    1. Christian ethics. 2. Theology, Practical. I. Title.

BJ1251 .R49 2012

In memory of my dad, William Edward Corbin (1933–2010)

Contents

Acknowledgments

THE IMPETUS FOR THIS book came from students I teach in a course at Ashland Theological Seminary, "Spiritual Formation and Social Activism." I have found students consistently eager to explore ethical issues through the prism of Christian spirituality, faith, and practice, and even more eager to find ways of bringing spiritual and moral formation together in concrete ways that serve the people of God and contribute to God's justice in the world. The organic connections they made between spiritual formation and ethics were encouraging and helpful for giving shape to the main ideas presented here. I hope they are helpful for those who choose to read this book.

I pass along my thanks to John Shultz, President of Ashland Theological Seminary, and my colleagues on the Faculty Development Committee for approving my request for study leave in the Spring of 2010 to start work on this manuscript. I did so while spending April at the Collegeville Institute for Ecumenical and Cultural Research at St. John's University in Collegeville, MN. What a place! I was warmly greeted and well tended to by Elisa Schneider. It was a wonderful opportunity that I hope comes my way again.

Colleagues and friends read portions of the manuscript. In the midst of their already busy schedules, I appreciate their willingness to take time to offer helpful suggestions. I solicited their contributions because I know firsthand how their lives are models of the relationships between Christian spirituality and morality. My thanks go to Lynn Karidis, Tom Snyder, and Jody Watson. It was an honor to have two previous students, graduates of Ashland Seminary, read and interact with the manuscript. Val Wysocki Hall and Matthew Williams read significant parts and made valuable contributions. I was privileged to receive their feedback and suggestions, which were incorporated at various places. A special acknowledgment goes to my graduate assistant, Polly Hitchcock, who read and responded to editorial queries in great detail and with a keen eye. I am thankful for the time she carved out to attend to the manuscript while already assisting me with courses and other projects, as well as attending to her own course work at seminary and various other responsibilities. Polly did a fantastic job and her input helped to clarify and strengthen sentences and syntax. Editor Charlie Collier and copy editor Jacob Martin provided needed direction and feedback at the crucial final stages of publication. Thanks to them are offered as well.

When seminary students interested in pursuing graduate work seek my advice, I remind them how important it is to stay grounded in a particular community of faith that can nurture them, keep them honest, and remind them of the larger purposes of their studies. I am so thankful to have such a faith community at Christ United Methodist Church in Ashland, Ohio. Mike and I are members of "God's Group" (a bold name indeed!). In Wesleyan fashion, our merry band meets together for study, prayer, service, worship, and accountability, all the while having lots of fun when we are together. I hope the following individuals know how dear they are to me and the formative role they have in my life: Rev. Kate Cox, Wayne Hathaway, Vicki and Ron Johnson, Bob and Pat Mansperger, Mary and Tom McNaull, Rev. Roger and Ellen Moore, Bea and Bruce North, Mike Reuschling, Janet Rockenfelder, Rev. Gordon and Jane Ruggles, and Wally Whitehouse and her dear husband, John, to whom we said goodbye in August 2011.

The day after I returned from my month in Minnesota, I received the phone call that every child fears to receive. My parents called to tell me my dad had received a dire cancer diagnosis that would be shortening his life. I got on a plane shortly thereafter to spend time with my parents. The time would come sooner than any one of us expected. My dad passed on May 28, 2010, in the way he wanted: at home, at peace, and ready to end this life in anticipation of the next one. We continue to grieve as an expression of the love we have for this husband, father, father-in-law, and Papa Corbin. And we do so together, finding new ways of being together and honoring my dad by attending to and maintaining our relationships. This book is dedicated to the memory of my dad, William Edward Corbin. It is also dedicated to those who remain and wait for the next Advent: my mom, Susan Corbin; my sister, Becky Kidd, brother-in-law, Bryan Kidd, and nephew, Will Riley; my brother, Bill Corbin; and my wonderful husband, Mike Reuschling.

Advent 2011

Introduction

I RETURNED TO THE United States in 1988 after four years of missionary service in Japan. Four years did not seem like a long time. Yet as I reentered church life after this absence, I felt a bit like Rip Van Winkle who had been asleep as an entire generation passed by. At church, there were many familiar faces and warm greetings; children had grown up; new members of the pastoral staff had been added; and improvements were made to the church building. However, the differences I noticed were not on the surface and not so immediately recognizable. The differences were in language, programming, ways of reading the Bible, and how one talked about a relationship with God.[1] Words and concepts such as spirituality were used in place of discipleship. Outreach came in the form of recovery groups. In sermons, the gospel was offered as healing for broken persons as well as necessary for salvation. Small group ministries existed to meet the various interests and needs of niche groups in order to provide safe environments for sharing and recovery from hurts. I had (re)entered a new cultural context.

Having intentionally lived cross-culturally and having studied mission and World Christianity in seminary, I was familiar with the dynamics of entering into unfamiliar cultural contexts and the necessities and challenges of contextualization. It is difficult to find words that express dynamic equivalence.[2] The need to find cultural forms for the expression of Christian faith and practice takes time, discernment, understanding, and thoughtfulness. Wrestling with the essentials of the gospel is important, requiring continual probing and reflection on what is essential to Christian

1. This observation on the shifts in language is made by Donnelly in "Prayer," 65. Donnelly notes that the shift in language also transforms our understanding of spiritual growth. For her this is not negative but instead an acknowledgment of the dynamic nature of spirituality, especially when engaged with the insights from disciplines such as psychology and sociology.

2. Dynamic equivalence is a mode of translation that seeks to find equivalence in language, idioms, and expressions between an original audience and a current one.

faith as opposed to peripheral. Living in ways that contextualize the gospel is an essential form of witness, informed by the embodiment of God's own self in the person of Christ and the diversity of the church's experiences in interpreting Scripture and aspiring to faithfulness throughout history. Yet I was unprepared for the ways in which these dynamics were taking shape in my white, middle-class, evangelical Protestant church context. Language was changing to contextualize new interests in spirituality as opposed to religiosity. The relational dimensions of Christian faith were highlighted over doctrinal commitments. All sorts of retreats and programs focusing on soul care and one's spiritual development were offered for those who could afford to attend them, those whose basic needs were met thanks to class location and economic privilege. This enabled attendees to focus on the "higher" dimensions of life, which were believed to be "the spiritual" as opposed to the material. The Sunday school class of which I was part was reading Larry Crabb's book *Inside Out*.[3] I remember the first conversation I had with one of the pastors upon my return. Over coffee, he wanted to know what I discovered about my inner child, areas of brokenness and need while I was in Japan. Perhaps because I had been with a bunch of missionary-activists and more pragmatically minded Christians for four years whose work was informed by deep piety and missional engagement, this question caught me off guard. I found it an odd question from a pastor, one who obviously fancied himself a bit of a psychologist.

Perhaps some of these trends I observed in the 1980s were important for correcting some of the one-sidedness of evangelical Christianity: an emphasis on doctrine over relationships; an insistence on Bible study as a key activity of small groups at the expense of sharing real-life issues and concerns; programs of discipleship geared toward information as opposed to spiritual formation; and the concern with preaching salvation as the primary task of the church, with meeting the real needs of people as secondary. These trends also reflected the sociological reality and need for religious groups to adapt and change in order to remain viable and relevant. These trends also were likely informed by the missional impetus characteristic of much of evangelical Christianity to "meet people where they're at" in order to share the gospel of Jesus Christ. It may have been the classic Pauline evangelistic adjustment of becoming "all things to all people, that I might by all means save some" (1 Cor 9:22–23).

3. Crabb, *Inside Out*.

Changes in religious communities and expressions are complex, multilayered, multicausal, and dynamic. Yet the changes I observed were not just cosmetic and contextual. They were also changes in how one understood the content of Christian faith, the nature and scope of spirituality, and the shape and purpose of the Christian life. I have had numerous opportunities to reflect on these changes over the last twenty years as an active church participant, on a church staff, and as a seminary professor. Attempting to articulate these changes and their implications is part of the motivation behind this book based on particular contexts and conversation partners over the years.

Contexts and Conversation Partners

The first time I read Richard Foster's book *Celebration of Discipline*, my initial thought was, "how legalistic."[4] I was raised in a Protestant context where the language of "spiritual disciplines" was fairly foreign. I suspect my preliminary reaction was also tinged with the unexamined caricature of works righteousness characteristic of the concerns of the early Protestant reformers. However, in spending more time with Foster, particularly his later works, *Freedom of Simplicity* and *Streams of Living Water*, my appreciation of the various expressions of Christian spirituality increased. This, coupled with a return to my Wesleyan roots, gave me a way to explain why I had always been drawn to the social justice streams of Christianity with a concern to ground works of justice in the love, mercy, compassion, and righteousness of God. This growing interest in the demands to do justice as part of Christian faith and practice was further solidified when I first read Stephen Mott's important work, *Biblical Ethics and Social Change*.[5] The biblical and theological foundations of justice were taking shape for me: justice is part of God's restoring work in the world, an integral aspect of the Kingdom of God, and an imperative response for those who have received the mercy and grace of God. My class in the Old Testament Prophets at Denver Seminary taught by Robert Hubbard was one of the most significant contexts for the formation of the ideas about justice I have today. Professor Hubbard's teaching and commitment to the call for justice inherent within Scripture and as part of what it means to claim covenant with God further increased my curiosity about the relationships between faith, "true

4. Foster, *Celebration of Discipline*.
5. Mott, *Biblical Ethics and Social Change*.

religion," spirituality, and justice. Justice was not just about ethics. It was about authentic faith.

While I was learning to read Scripture in ways that highlighted its social dimensions, and as I was exploring the implications of Christian faith in such areas as economic, racial, gender and social justice, I became increasingly puzzled by the split maintained between evangelism and social justice in the contexts in which I was working and worshipping. There was an underlying assumption that a person's greatest need was spiritual. This need was met through evangelism, through a presentation of the gospel, given so that a person might respond to its invitation of salvation and eternal life. When I pressed for expressions of the gospel that were concrete and focused on the material needs of persons, I was often castigated for being "liberal." It was liberals as opposed to evangelicals who were concerned about justice, which was perceived as a peripheral concern of the gospel. At times there were concessions made that perhaps social justice ministries were important—but only as they gave opportunity to share the gospel, which clearly involved an evangelistic message to those who had come for a meal and warm shower. I could never figure out how this strategy was different from emotional manipulation and exploitation of a person's basic needs for food, shelter, clothing, health care, or employment to accomplish another objective. What of our own faithful response to God's initiation of grace and compassion and the teaching of Jesus to "go and do likewise?" (Luke 10:37).

I was further perplexed by the selectivity of moral concerns and a growing spiritualization of Christian faith that ignored its communal and social dimensions. It is unfair to say there was no social activism in some evangelical contexts starting in the late 1970s and continuing to today. With the US Supreme Court decision in *Roe v. Wade* in 1973, which overturned state laws prohibiting abortion, evangelicals were propelled into public involvement, forming grassroots movements and calling on elected leaders to work rigorously to overturn *Roe v. Wade*. Yet it is fair to say that much of the social concern expressed by evangelicals has been limited to such issues as abortion and sexuality.[6] In spite of the persistent work of Jim Wallis, the work of Sojourners, "The Chicago Declaration of Evangelical Social Concern" in 1973, and the subsequent founding of Evangelicals for Social Action by Ron Sider, only recently have evangelicals become involved with speaking out against more varied social ethical issues. Now on the radar

6. Corbin, "Moral Selectivity."

screen are issues such as human trafficking, the degradation of the environment, torture, and poverty, concerns informed by Scripture, energized by faith, and spurred on by God's love for all persons and desire for justice.[7] It is heartening to see the recovery of a more robust and broad social conscience and engagement characteristic of early expressions of American evangelicalism in the eighteenth and nineteenth centuries.[8]

The growing spiritualization of Christian faith has also been a development that troubles me. Samuel Powell identifies this as an "abstract spirituality," a "notion that worship is mainly an act of inwardness and that does not require physical or public acts."[9] His insights are applicable to spirituality broadly conceived and practiced, which has been overly personalized and interiorized. I do believe that our lives as Christians have deeply spiritual dimensions, if by this we mean an invitation from the Trinitarian God to participate in God's own life, empowered by the Holy Spirit, being formed more and more into the likeness of Jesus Christ. This truly is a call and gift from a transcendent God and prepares us for living a life truly connected with and grounded in the Source beyond ourselves.

Yet this invitation from God does not happen in some ethereal sphere. This invitation has come to us in Christ, the very incarnation of God. It comes to us now even as we wait for the full redemption and restoration of God's creation and the resurrection of our bodies. It is a spiritualiz*ing* tendency that causes me concern. By spiritualizing I mean the process of either reducing the Christian life to *just* spiritual matters, or overly privatizing and interiorizing spiritual formation to *just* one's own inward growth.[10] A spiritualizing faith privileges one aspect of our life, that which is allegedly "spiritual," while minimizing the very real, material, and embodied dimensions of life that are crucial to what it means to be created by God, and how to live as a creature before God and in relationship with others. While there is no shortage of conversations about spirituality, I find myself wondering if there are any differences between our current conceptions of spirituality and early gnosticism, which denigrated bodily life and relegated spiritual

---

7. See the following Web sites: www.sojo.net; www.esa-online.org; and www.evangelicalsforhumanrights.org.

8. See the good historical overview by Dayton, *Discovering an Evangelical Heritage.*

9. Powell, *Theology of Christian Spirituality*, 100.

10. For a more sustained critique of these tendencies, see chapter 4 of my book *Reviving Evangelical Ethics.*

insight to a privileged space for a privileged few.[11] Does this kind of "abstract spirituality" and spiritualizing make a difference for how one actually lives and engages with the concrete realities and moral concerns of life?

I entered my doctoral program in Christian social ethics at Drew University with many of these questions and concerns in mind. My program was interdisciplinary in nature in that while my focus was Christian social ethics, courses in the sociology and psychology of religion were required as part of my program. It was through the insights of sociologists of religion that I began to understand what I had observed about the language of spirituality, its expressions, and its actual function in communities and individual lives. With my earliest reading of *Habits of the Heart* while in seminary, to exposure to sociologists of religion while in graduate school and beyond, I was beginning to recognize aspects of my own faith tradition through a different set of lenses, often in very uncomfortable ways.[12] These perspectives further shaped my interests in topics related to spirituality. Because my primary discipline is Christian social ethics, I am geared more toward the normative dimensions of faith and how they are expressed in decisions, actions, and practices. It is here that my interests in spirituality and morality intersect, and what drives the questions and concerns of this book. How does Christian belief and practice provide normative criteria (ethical dimensions) to guide and give shape to our conceptions of spirituality? How do our spiritual practices change and shape us (formational dimensions) to live lives of integrity and wholeness in light of the moral demands of our world? How are spiritual practices morally forming, and how do ethical practices reflect authentic spirituality?

Why This Book?

There is no shortage of books on spirituality or on Christian ethics. So, why another book? And will this one be any different? Even though this book is written with these experiences and observations in mind, it is informed by a number of questions and subsequent convictions that will become clear in the chapters that follow. I remain unsettled and uneasy with three related dynamics I have experienced in certain forms of evangelical Protestant practices of spirituality: its overly interiorized emphasis, its disconnection from Christian moral formation, and the lack of concern for social justice

11. See Cooper, *Life in the Flesh*.

12. See Bellah et al., *Habits of the Heart*.

as a matter for spiritual and moral formation. I share the thesis of Richard Gula that *"spirituality without morality is disembodied; morality without spirituality is rootless."*[13] These questions and concerns give shape to the structure of this book in the following ways.

In chapters 1 through 3, I will bring insights offered on spiritual and moral formation from a variety of sources. Although the work of one person, this book will reflect various perspectives on spirituality and morality, eventually bringing them together to explore how spiritual and moral formation are related and necessary for Christian faith. In chapter 1, I will explore the content, contours, and direction of spiritual formation based on scriptural and theological paradigms as primary prisms through which to understand Christian spirituality. My hope is to offer a conception of spirituality in a theological framework important for defining its content, shape, and the trajectories on which it places us in learning to live faithfully with God and others. I will focus on moral formation in chapter 2 based on contributions from Christian ethics and moral psychology. I will bring the insights on spirituality and morality together for an integrative proposal on their relationship in chapter 3. I will work to respect the distinctiveness of these domains so that spiritual formation is not collapsed into moral formation and vice versa. While I recognize they are not the same, I do believe there are important relationships and similar dynamics, particularly for Christians. Powell also affirms that "the spiritual life of Christians, whether in the form of devotional exercises or expressly ethical activity in the world, is the Christian faith in one of its forms, the form of lived-out activity, just as belief in the Christian faith is another form, the form of cognitive affirmation."[14] How spirituality and morality are related, and the implications for attending to both kinds of formation as essential for the faithful and dynamic living out of Christian faith, will be the core of this chapter.

In chapters 4, 5, and 6, I will utilize this integrative understanding of spiritual and moral formation in an exploration of concrete practices I suggest are both spiritually forming and ethically necessary. Instead of talking about spiritual and ethical practices in separate chapters, I will devote each chapter to an exploration of the relationship between a spiritual and ethical practice. I have chosen three spiritual disciplines—prayer, simplicity, and confession—and three ethical practices—speaking out, consuming,

13. Gula, *Call to Holiness*, 5. Italics in original.

14. Powell, *Theology of Christian Spirituality*, 9.

and resistance. The reader may recognize a parallel in the spiritual disciplines I have chosen to Richard Foster's typologies of "inward, outward and corporate" in *Celebration of Discipline* where he situates prayer as inward, simplicity as outward, and confession as corporate and upward.[15] While I appreciate the need to "type" and organize material into categories, typologies must also be blurry and porous lest they solidify and reify categories as givens. I do not think this was Foster's intent, yet I fear that in actual practice, prayer is perceived and practiced as *just* inward, simplicity as *merely* outward, and confession as *only* upward. This, in my mind, has further reinforced the divorce between spirituality and morality, so that spirituality becomes "who" we are and morality "what" we do. This is why I will not employ Foster's categories but will argue that spiritual disciplines and ethical practices are always private and public, and personal and social. The ethical practices I have chosen—speaking out, consumption practices, and resistance—are ones in which I am interested and ones that I think have been neglected as part of prophetic Christian faith. They are important because they impinge on how we attend to the needs of others, how we exercise our faith commitments based on what we believe about God's relationship to the world, our involvement in it, and our responsibilities for others as concerns of both spirituality and morality. As mentioned, I will not explore these as separate practices but as linked to and integrated with our spiritual disciplines of prayer, simplicity, and confession.

It's important to say more about practices since this is central to the chapters on integrating spirituality and morality. The important work on Christian practices by Dorothy Bass and Craig Dykstra have deeply informed my commitments and work.[16] Their work and the influence of Alasdair MacIntyre on the recovery of virtue in Christian ethics have been important for realizing the role of practices, their social dimensions, and their extension of the narrative of Scripture and Christian faith.[17] The definition of practices proposed by Bass and Dykstra as "things Christian people do together over time to address fundamental human needs in response to and in light of God's active presence for the life of the world"

15. Foster, *Celebration of Discipline*.

16. See the following: Bass and Dykstra, *For Life Abundant*; Volf and Bass, *Practicing Theology*; Bass, *Practicing Our Faith*.

17. MacIntyre, *After Virtue*. For the influence of MacIntyre on Christian virtue ethics, see the following: Hauerwas, *Community of Character*; Hauerwas and Pinches, *Christians Among the Virtues*; Kotva, *Christian Case for Virtue Ethics*; and Murphy, Kallenberg, and Nation, *Virtues and Practices in the Christian Tradition*.

provides a point of reference for how I will articulate the relationships between spiritual and moral practices.[18] MacIntyre's definition of a practice is "any coherent and complex form of socially established cooperative human activity through which goods internal to that form of activity are realized in the course of trying to achieve those standards of excellence which are appropriate to, and partially definitive of, that form of activity, with the result that human powers to achieve excellence, and human conceptions of the ends and goods involved, are systematically extended."[19] While MacIntyre does not offer an explicitly theological conception or Christian narration of practices, his definition highlights important dimensions. Practices are social and cooperative human activities that train persons in how to live what they believe and, in so doing, make a profound impact on the lives of other persons, including those performing the practice. What is crucial to note in both definitions of practices are their social dimensions, and their relationships to narratives, the means of formation, and the impact they have on both practitioners and receivers. These very social and public dimensions of practices are important for understanding the relationship between spirituality and morality. I will elaborate more on these definitions and how I will use them in subsequent chapters when discussing spiritual and ethical practices.

I also realize the complexity of practices. This book does not provide a comprehensive definition of prayer, simplicity, and confession, followed by seamless and simple implications for speaking out, consuming, and resisting. Something like prayer is far too complex, multifaceted, and traditioned to do this, and speaking out, because it is contingent on moral context, requires discernment and analysis of the various layers of a *particular* moral issue. I recognize the need for "thickness" in descriptions of practices, especially due to the limits and influences of my own location.[20] In light of this, I will talk about particular aspects of prayer, simplicity, and confession, realizing there is far more to say about these important spiritual disciplines. I will resist trying to be prescriptive and overly simplistic in my judgments and what I offer, things that are difficult for a Christian social ethicist.

---

18. Dykstra and Bass, "Theological Understanding of Christian Practices," 18.

19. MacIntyre, *After Virtue*, 187.

20. I am using "thickness" in the way suggested by Geertz in *Interpretation of Cultures*, 14. Geertz proposes that any ethnographic and anthropological descriptions of groups must account for their "thickness" given the complexity of cultural contexts and their influence on behavior, interpretation, and meaning.

So I end with a confession based on Kathryn Tanner's suggestion. To insist "that Christian practices are much more prescriptively rule-bound than other comparably complex practices—is to be less than fully cognizant of human fallibility before a finally unapproachable Truth that is God's alone."[21] Yet this is why practices require "critical theological engagement," since "in order to figure out how to go on, one must, with some measure of reflective exertion, figure out the meaning of what one has been doing, why one does it, and what it implies—in particular, how it hangs together (or fails to hang together) with the rest of what one believes and does."[22] So, I go on, proceeding with an appropriate awareness of the limitations of this book, but with hope that what I offer based on theological and moral reflection might help us connect spiritual disciplines such as prayer, simplicity, and confession with speaking out about what might be true about God, what God cares about in human communities, and what is "noble, right, pure, lovely, admirable and excellent," in order to put these things into practice (Phil 4:8–9).

21. Tanner, "Theological Reflection and Christian Practices," 231. See also the helpful article by Brown, "Exploring the Text/Practice Interface."

22. Tanner, "Theological Reflection and Christian Practices," 232.

one

Desiring Right Things

AFTER GRADUATING FROM COLLEGE in 1979, I worked for a time in human resources at a bank. One of my coworkers had crystals and other religious items at her desk. She had moved to Boulder, Colorado, because it was a mecca of sorts for all things spiritual. There were numerous stores in the business of selling items and trinkets believed to enhance one's spirituality, as well as Eastern meditation centers, alternative religious gathering places (meaning alternative to Christianity and Judaism), and an overall mystical aura due to the beautiful setting of this city at the base of the Flatirons in the foothills of the Rocky Mountains. My coworker was raised in the context of Jewish faith, but her primary point of reference for finding meaning to her life was not her religious tradition but her various eclectic practices of spirituality. In other words, she was spiritual but not religious.[1]

Before exploring Christian spirituality from scriptural and theological perspectives, it is first important to identify the trajectories that created the furrows of difference between religion and spirituality that mark much of our landscape today. There are three trails to briefly follow that illuminate how we got here, which, in turn, may help us find ways forward in order to recover the relationships between spirituality and morality so vital to Christian faith. These paths are historical and hence epistemological, theological, and sociological in nature.

How We Got Here: A Very Brief Jaunt

One does not have to be schooled in postmodern thought to recognize the seismic shifts that have occurred in how one perceives reality, ascertains

1. Schneiders, "Religion vs. Spirituality," 163–85.

1

and describes what is truthful, responds to the sacred, and articulates the meaning and purpose of one's life. These epistemological changes occurred over a long period of time and simultaneously with the rise of the sciences as means of discovering what is truthful. Coincidentally, we have witnessed the growing suspicion of religious institutions and clerical power, emerging social reforms that resulted in legal rights and more democratic forms of government, as well as the expansion of Western ideas of individualism along with economic and political power to various parts of the world. This has impacted how one understands and relates to God, self, creation, and other human beings and has shaped our understandings about the content, purpose, and practice of religious faith. Dennis Billy and James Keating describe certain historical movements in Western Christianity that led to the gradual separation between faith and conscience, and the unmooring of morality from one's religious training, beliefs, and practices.[2] As morality came under the purview of philosophy, particularly in the Enlightenment forms that elevated the role of human reason, it was gradually removed from the authority and practices of the church, and hence from its theological underpinnings. Spirituality became privatized and interiorized, even as morality became a matter of one's own conscience that was developed apart from the suspicious and heternomous influences of religion, particularly religion mediated by clergy and ecclesiastical institutions.[3]

The shift in views about clerical authority and the interpretation and exercise of religious faith propelled Protestant reformers—Luther and Calvin, among others—to respond to certain abuses they perceived in medieval Catholicism. They reacted to the theological incoherence they perceived between the Bible and the Church's interpretation, especially in matters of faith, works, the sacraments, and salvation, as well as the economic and political hegemony exercised by the Magisterium. While I do not wish to simplify the multiple and interlocking social, political, and theological dynamics of the Reformation and its diversity, there was one hallmark that identified the concerns of the Reformers and continues to characterize much of Protestantism today. It is the collection of *solas*: *sola fides*, *sola*

---

2. Billy and Keating, *Conscience and Prayer*, chapter 1.

3. This move was made by Immanuel Kant, who believed that ethics must be grounded in human reason, not religion, since reason was common to all humans, making the search for the Categorical Imperative possible. Religion, on the other hand, was an external influence that prohibited the exercise of reason, and therefore should be rejected as a source of morality. For a more extended conversation on Kant and a Christian ethical perspective, see chapter 1 of my *Reviving Evangelical Ethics*.

gratia, sola scriptura, sola Christo, and *soli Deo Gloria.* The impact of these emphases of "only" on Protestant spirituality and ethics, according to Samuel Powell, has resulted in a difficulty in maintaining an important dialogic between faith and works organic to Christian faith since "faith contains an ethical dimension" that must not be ignored.[4] However, as "faith alone" was emphasized, the moves to precise articulations of doctrinal content came to characterize certain wings of the Reformation, with the pendulum swinging to the side of justification solely by faith in response to what was perceived to be "works righteousness." While the content of Christian faith is extremely important, as I will argue later in this chapter, the elevation of right belief embedded in well-defined doctrines tended to minimize the equally important implications of faith for how one lives in light of what one believes and how theological claims inform one's experience. This unintended split, as a polemic response to the priority of faith over works, has had unfortunate effects in sustaining the relationship between belief and practice, faith and works, and spirituality and morality in various forms of Protestantism.

Revivalistic expressions of Christianity—particularly in the United States, according to Powell—have been responses to sterilized views of faith, which limit the Christian life to a rational adherence to doctrinal claims. The constraining of belief to cognitive assent to theological propositions resulted in a pendulum swing to "excessive spiritualization of faith" that exhibits itself in such things as a "highly individualistic devotional quality, in which the sum of religion consists in the individual's relation to Jesus," and an emphasis on "a certain kind of emotional experience and individual focus at the center of the Christian life, an experience and a focus that do not, in themselves, encourage a profound involvement with the world."[5] While ethics in a spiritualized faith may be important, its shape is primarily individualistic and interior, and it often takes negative forms in terms of avoiding certain behaviors and questionable company. Spirituality tends also to be privileged as the most important aspect of human experience and fosters an inordinate amount of attention to one's own spiritual well-being at the expense of the actual well-being of others.

This "spiritualization of faith" is a development described by sociologists of religion based on their observations and analysis of the role of religious faith and spirituality in the United States. Of particular note is Robert

4. Powell, *Theology of Christian Spirituality,* 76.
5. Ibid., 78–83.

Wuthnow's analysis in *After Heaven: Spirituality in America since the 1950s*.[6] Wuthnow observes the movement from a spirituality of dwelling to a spirituality of seeking. A spirituality of dwelling is associated with traditional places of worship such as churches, synagogues, and mosques—places that were important in one's family and neighborhood. A spirituality of dwelling includes prescribed religious practices learned in catechisms and reinforced in formal liturgies and church practices. However, a spirituality of seeking ceases to attach significant meaning to these more traditional ways of learning about God and interacting with the sacred. This new kind of spirituality has been shaped by the massive shifts in American culture since the 1950s: the growing distrust of institutions, the rising emphasis on freedom as self-expression, the power of the market to shape desires and choices, the gradual decline of mainline churches and the rise of grassroots evangelical movements, and the increasing mobility of Americans moving from cities to suburbs or across the country for employment and other opportunities. According to Wuthnow, the result has been "a growing awareness that spirituality and organized religion are quite different, and, indeed, may run in opposite directions."[7] Two particular effects are also important to note. With the upsurge of interest in spirituality, especially in popular print and other media, "subjectivity was elevated as a central concern, opening the way for increased attention to the interior life," while "intentional action toward social or personal transformation was often implicitly devalued."[8]

However, a spirituality of dwelling ought not to be pitted against a spirituality of seeking, according to Wuthnow. In reference to the Benedictine tradition, "dwelling and seeking are both part of what it means to be human."[9] Persons need "home," connections with others and traditions that orient and ground us. Yet the inability to encapsulate God in any one tradition, place, or perspective keeps us pushing forward in the search for

6. Wuthnow, *After Heaven*.

7. Ibid., 72.

8. Ibid., 78–79.

9. Ibid., 6. I spent a good portion of my time writing this book at the Collegeville Institute for Ecumenical and Cultural Research at St. John's University in Collegeville, Minnesota. Both St. John's and St. Benedict's model these truths: beautiful dwellings and space that connect us with a place, tradition, and spiritual practices, as well as a seeking that is open to various perspectives, God's work in the world, and how we ought to participate in God's good work on behalf of the world. See the Collegeville Institute's Web site: www.collegevilleinstitute.org.

meaning, authenticity, and always better and more faithful ways of relating to God and others. As Wuthnow notes, an alternative to the gap between dwelling and seeking is a recovery of spiritual practices that reconnect spirituality with its moral dimensions and concrete ways of living in the world because of what one believes. He writes:

> Spiritual practices put responsibility squarely on individuals to spend time on a regular basis worshiping, communing with, listening to, and attempting to understand the ultimate source of sacredness in their lives. Spiritual practices can be performed in the company of others, and they are inevitably embedded in religious institutions, but they must also be performed individually if they are to be personally meaningful and enriching. Spiritual practices require individuals to engage reflectively in a conversation with their past, examining who they have been, how they have been shaped, and where they are headed. Spiritual practices have a moral dimension, for they instruct people in how they should behave toward themselves and with each other, but these practices are also an item of faith, encouraging people to walk each day with partial knowledge and in cautious hope.[10]

I find this emphasis on spiritual practices hopeful for finding a way to bridge the gap between spirituality and morality, which is my primary concern in this book. I will say more about practices later, but first it is important to reconnect spirituality and morality before exploring practices as important points of intersection between the two. In this chapter, I will begin to build this bridge by focusing on the direction and content of Christian spirituality and spiritual formation. I will do so by focusing on desire for the right things (spirituality) and reach over to right things to desire (morality) in the next chapter.

Desiring the Right Things

Before exploring Christian spirituality as it relates to desiring the right things, it is important to articulate how I see the relationship between spirituality and spiritual formation since I will move back and forth in my use of these terms. Sandra Schneiders describes spirituality as a characteristic of the human being, "the capacity of persons to transcend themselves through knowledge and love, that is, to reach beyond themselves in relationship

---

10. Wuthnow, *After Heaven*, 16.

to others and thus become more than self-enclosed material monads."[11] Spirituality is fueled by a desire to find meaning and coherence in one's life, which requires "conscious involvement in the project of life-integration through self-transcendence toward the ultimate value one perceives."[12] So while spirituality is more connotative of experience, it does involve values, understandings of ultimate goods, and perceptions of the nature and purpose of transcendence. Spirituality is nurtured and oriented by visions of life and desires we see as ultimate and worthy of pursuit—those that enhance our awareness of our humanity as well as of the sacred. From a Christian perspective, spirituality ought to be experienced in and fostered by a dynamic relationship with the Trinitarian God, which requires degrees of clarity about who God is, how God relates to the world, and what God ultimately desires for creation as key foci for orienting desires and practices.[13] Schneiders goes on to elaborate: "the horizon of ultimate value is the triune God revealed in Jesus Christ in whose life we share through the gift of the Holy Spirit. Christian spirituality is the life of faith, hope, and love within the community of the Church through which we put on the mind of Christ by participating sacramentally and existentially in his paschal mystery. The desired life-integration is personal transformation in Christ, which implies participation in the transformation of the world in justice for all creatures."[14]

At the heart of Christian spirituality is the notion of desire for life-integration based on "*ultimate* loves—that to which we are fundamentally oriented, what ultimately governs our vision of the good life, what shapes and molds our being-in-the-world—in other words, what we desire above all else, the ultimate desire that shapes and positions and makes sense of all our penultimate desires and actions."[15] Desire is "the heart of all spirituality"

11. Schneiders, "Religion vs. Spirituality," 165.

12. Ibid., 166.

13. See the recent volume *Dictionary of Christian Spirituality*, edited by Scorgie et al., for rich descriptions and overviews of Christian spirituality.

14. Schneiders, "Religion vs. Spirituality," 168.

15. Smith, *Desiring the Kingdom*, 51. Italics in original. Smith is recovering the Augustinian notion of desire and develops an anthropology that describes humans as "liturgical animals" who orient our lives around ultimate loves and visions of how the world ought to be that are embodied in practices. Smith's focus is on the "education of desire" (23), particularly in the context of higher Christian education. His insights are very helpful for (re)conceiving formation in all sorts of contexts, particularly in seminaries and churches.

and "embodies the sense that humanity has a longing that can only be satisfied in God."[16] Christian spiritual formation involves processes, practices, and ways of integrating our lives by embodying our commitments to ultimate desires.[17] Spiritual formation is a process of learning to live out in concrete form and in particular situations the values, goods, and ultimate purposes of Christian faith, which is relationship with God and faithful participation in the life and work of God in the world. It is opening ourselves to the process of being formed, changed, and directed by the Spirit into ways of living wherein what we believe is more and more integrated and manifested in what we care about, what we pursue, what we love, how we live, and who we understand ourselves to be. Spiritual formation is about discerning right things in a world of competing visions of the good life and competing conceptions of wholeness and holiness that shape, tug, and pull our desires in multiple directions, often away from God and God's desires for human life.[18]

Desires inform our affections, another key concept in spirituality and morality. Desire—that which we ultimately long for—shapes our affections, those "dispositions and character traits that are grown in believers' hearts as they move toward being like Christ."[19] Affections are visible expressions of the One we love and what we love that guide how we act and the choices we make. It's important to differentiate between affections and feelings, given highly experiential and emotional expressions in popular spirituality today. While not discounting the important role of feelings and emotions in human experience, as necessary for passionate expressions in spirituality and morality, William Spohn suggests that

> It is important to distinguish the affections from feelings. *Feelings* are transitory occurrences that may be genuine or not. The affections behind the Christian moral life are not simply spontaneous, like feelings. They can be tutored and evoked, for example, by the language of prayer or the rhythm of ritual. They can also be

16. Sheldrake, "Desire," 231.

17. See Brown, Dahl, and Corbin Reuschling, *Becoming Whole and Holy*, for an integrative approach to spiritual formation. See also the following sources for various perspectives on Christian spirituality and formation: Greenman and Kalantzis, *Life in the Spirit*; and Holder, *Blackwell Companion to Christian Spirituality*.

18. See Cavanaugh, *Being Consumed*, for an interesting exploration of the Augustinian notion of desire in light of how our desires to consume are shaped by a market economy.

19. Elliott, "Affections," 248.

deliberately shaped by specific practices like hospitality, caring for the sick, sharing possessions, and forgiveness. These actions may first be done out of a sense of obligation, but over time they should evoke the dispositions of generosity, compassion, and justice. They become "second nature" to the maturing disciple.[20]

Spohn's point is that affections can be shaped and "tutored" in ways that feelings cannot, given the spontaneous and often momentary responses that feelings provoke. For Spohn, "Affections lead to corresponding actions, and that roots them more deeply in the character."[21] Psychologist Robert Roberts, while perhaps sharing Spohn's concern about the spontaneity of emotions, has a higher place for emotions, which he describes as "concern-based construals" that "can be expressions of character traits: emotions are based on concerns, some concerns are passions, and passions are character traits, on-going master concerns that deeply characterize a person. . . . The emotions that are . . . shaped by the good news of the gospel—joy, gratitude, hope, contrition, peace, compassion—are the fruit of the Holy Spirit and express Christian character."[22] While emotions and feelings are natural parts of the human experience, and are important ways in which we connect with the experiences of others, affections go much deeper and offer us a way to sustain our pursuit of desire when feelings do diminish and passion ebbs and flows. Desires inform affections, while affections help us order feelings and passions as we seek to bring all of our lives in alignment with a desire for deeper relationship with God and a more faithful living out of what we believe.

Spiritual formation is a continual process of shaping, reshaping, orienting, and reorienting our desires and affections for God, who is forming us more and more into the image of Jesus Christ through the ongoing work of the Holy Spirit as we pursue and practice what our Ultimate Desire requires. For Christians, the content of God's desires and the direction this provides for spirituality are guided by the Scriptures, which offer us a narrative context *and* content crucial for spiritual formation. Schneiders suggests that "authentic spirituality is biblical in some sense, and all salvific engagement with the Bible (as opposed to a purely secular, scientific

---

20. Spohn, *Go and Do Likewise*, 41. Italics in original.

21. Ibid.

22. Roberts, *Spiritual Emotions*, 20. See also chapter 1 in Saliers, *Soul in Paraphrase*, for a helpful discussion on religious affections and emotions.

study of the text as history or literature) shapes and nourishes spirituality."[23] Scripture fosters authentic spirituality in three primary ways, according to Schneiders. First, Scripture offers a variety of spiritualities that have shaped the various spiritual expressions and commitments across Christian traditions.[24] She suggests that

> The variety of biblical spiritualities in scripture legitimates, and provides resources for, the variety of spiritualities among Christians throughout the ages and in various settings. Protestant and Catholic and Orthodox, familial and monastic, contemplative and prophetic, socially committed and mystical, Benedictine and Ignatian, Lutheran and Presbyterian, liturgical and devotional, feminist and pacifist spiritualities can all find criteria for discernment and resources for growth in the Bible. None of these spiritualities is exclusive, and a healthy Christian spirituality involves overlapping strands even as it manifests dominant tendencies.[25]

Second, Scripture provides a pattern for Christian living that is rooted in and flows from a relationship with the God of Scripture.[26] Finally, Schneiders proposes that biblical spirituality must involve "*a transformative process of personal and communal engagement with the biblical text.*"[27] She is concerned about the divorce between serious study of Scripture and religious experience, leaving experience bereft of substance and overly personalized while removing study from the context of Christian faith and practice.[28] I share these concerns about a contentless and contextless spirituality and a vapid reading and use of Scripture that lacks imagination and understanding of the relationship between spirituality and our moral sensibilities that are inherent in the scriptural witness and required for faithful Christian living. The result is that we look elsewhere for our

---

23. Schneiders, "Biblical Spirituality," 134. See also Humphrey, *Ecstasy and Intimacy*, for a fabulous articulation of the biblical/theological narratives and historical perspectives on Christian spirituality.

24. Schneiders, "Biblical Spirituality," 134.

25. Ibid., 135.

26. Ibid.

27. Ibid., 136. Italics in original.

28. I often remind students who think that seminary education, particularly work in biblical studies and theology, has little to do with their devotional life and spiritual formation, that according to Richard Foster, study is a spiritual discipline, in that the life of the mind is crucial for understanding, discerning, and pursuing what we should desire. See chapter 5 in Foster's *Celebration of Discipline*.

spiritual experiences and often seek them outside of a vibrant and growing relationship with Christ and others. We also develop our Christian ethic with little reference to a relationship with God, Scripture, the teachings of the church, and our faith commitments. We end up widening the divide between spirituality and morality by unhinging from both Scripture and tradition, leaving experience "out there" with little stable point of reference. There is an important dialectic between experience and study, so that one informs the other and both are needed for an authentic Christian spirituality that requires "ultimate horizons" and "basic coordinates" offered by Scripture, theology, Christian community, liturgical practices, ministry, and mission.[29] Since "Scripture is not only a record of the spirituality of our forebears but a source and pattern of our spirituality," it is appropriate to attend to Scripture in my exploration of spirituality and morality, particularly on the content, context, and shaping of desire.[30]

Desiring God and the Things of God

Christian spirituality starts with and is propelled forward by discernment and desire, particularly the desire for God and the things of God. Scripture is replete with images of negative and positive desires. One of the starkest contrasts between these opposing kinds of desire is found in Paul's letter to the Christians of Galatia. The contrast Paul presents in Galatians 5:16–26 is between the desires of the sinful nature and the desires of the Spirit. Galatians is one of Paul's harshest letters to early churches. After his normal salutation (Gal 1:1–5), Paul launches right into naming his concerns about the cluster of churches in Galatia, starting with his main concern that they have turned to a "different gospel—which is really no gospel at all" (1:6–7). There is no commendation for this group of Christians, since turning to a different gospel was a fundamental denial of the revelation of Christ (1:11–12), justification by grace (2:15–17), and freedom from the law (3:1–14). The "different gospel" is propagated by "certain people" or teachers, who receive the harshest of condemnations from Paul in the form of a curse (1:7–9).

Paul's letter to the Galatians presents a series of contrasts that take us to the contrast between the desires of the flesh and those of the Spirit.[31]

29. Schneiders, "Biblical Spirituality," 134.

30. Ibid., 141.

31. Gaventa, "Galatians."

The first of these is the "fundamental contrast . . . between the law and Christ."[32] From this seminal contrast flow others: between faith and obedience to the law (3:1–14); between the old covenant and the new (3:15–25); between heirs of God and slaves (3:26—4:7), illustrated by the difference between Hagar and Sarah (4:21–31); between freedom in Christ and slavery (5:1–15); and, finally, between the desires of the flesh and the life of the Spirit (5:16–26).

How might we understand this contrast between the desires of the flesh and the fruit of the Spirit in Galatians 5:16–26 for grounding Christian spirituality in its scriptural context? Given that codes of virtues were common in ancient moral philosophy, what makes this particular list of good and bad desires that Christians are exhorted to pursue (or avoid) more "Christian" in substance, purpose, and direction? The theological context is important for properly understanding Christian spirituality so that it does not become a Christianized version of the stoic denial of desire and mortification of the flesh, something entirely dependent on human striving. The framework for Paul's exhortation to "live by the Spirit" (5:16) is the life, death, and resurrection of Christ. It is justification by faith, our being received as daughters and sons of God, our incorporation into Christ's body and our new identities, the gift of the Spirit, and God's new creation that guide the kinds of desires we are to pursue and the lives we are to live. Paul is not proposing a dualistic theological anthropology by contrasting the flesh and the Spirit, lest we assume that our bodies are either flesh or spirit. We are not gnostic spiritualists who denigrate the body in favor of a higher form of spirituality that ignores the material dimensions of our lives in Christ. Instead, we are "new *creations*" (6:15, italics mine) who now live according to the newness of the Spirit in all areas of our embodied existence because of what Christ has done in his body, and because of his subsequent bodily resurrection.

This flesh and spirit dualism is important to Paul's ethic, according to John Barclay. This dualism is not an ontological statement that reduces humans to flesh or spirit and therefore cannot be used to support some kind of dichotomy of the human being. Instead, "Paul uses the Spirit-flesh dualism here as a framework within which to present his moral instructions . . . [F]lesh' and 'Spirit' thus designate two alternative ways of life and imply distinct ethical practices."[33] "Flesh" in this context is *sarx*, often

32. Ibid., 1377.
33. Barclay, *Obeying the Truth*, 178.

a metaphorical description of sinful nature pursuing wayward desires and "the tendency in the human person to live an existence completely and totally centered on the self."[34] It is important to note that "flesh" is not the same thing as "body." It is not the "body" in which Paul locates the impetus for sinful desires so destructive to spirituality and community. Instead, it is something far more inherent in the human tendency to focus on and exalt the self so as to pursue longings and desires outside a context of relationship with Christ, and outside the responsibilities of Christian community.

There is an ironic twist here for conceptions of spirituality that are pursued and practiced with highly individualistic tones. If *sarx* is descriptive of our human tendency for a self-centered existence and out-of-proportion attention to one's self, one can still be "fleshly" if spirituality is overly self-focused and interiorized, the aim being self-discovery and fulfillment at the expense of attention and care for other selves. In contrast, Spohn writes that authentic spirituality is other centered. He writes:

> Spirituality is concerned not only with acts that are explicitly related to God but with the more pervasive awareness of God expressed by Ignatian spirituality as "finding God in all things." Its practices are not only interior; rather, they integrate bodily actions and public commitments with convictions that are rooted in the person's affective and cognitive structure. Authentic spirituality is not confined to an individualistic "care of the soul," since its practices and frame of reference are communally based and oriented to action with and for others. In the framework of the story of Jesus, a spirituality that is purely inward and unrelated to moral transformation and action must be considered unauthentic.[35]

So while spiritual formation occurs in the body, its aim is the reshaping and continual shaping of desires, our deepest affections, which are informed by either the flesh or the Spirit, determining how we live in our bodies and in relationship with others. What Paul means by "desire" in Galatians has two directions. Desires, *epithumian*, are those core longings that can take a positive, wholesome, and life-giving direction, such as the desires of the Spirit that form us according to God's desires for our lives. Or they can take the direction of craving and covetousness—desires that are essentially insatiable, unwholesome, and destructive to self and to communities. In Christian moral thought, discerning the differences between

34. Matera, *Galatians*, 196.
35. Spohn, *Go and Do Likewise*, 36.

rightly ordered and disordered desires is important for spirituality and morality. These differences are apparent and magnified by the contrasts that Paul makes between the desires of the sinful flesh (disordered) and the desires of the Spirit (rightly ordered desires). Desires are rightly ordered by the love of God and what God loves, which are human beings, right relationships, restoration, and wholeness in all of God's creation. Since God exists as three persons in perfect harmony and union, redemptively existing and working on behalf of the world, what God desires is what Jesus patterns for us and what the Spirit makes possible. What the Spirit desires is therefore what God desires: love, joy, peace, patience, kindness, generosity, faithfulness, gentleness, and self-control (Gal 5:22–23). It is good to desire these fruits, and to "produce" them out of relationships with God, with and *for* others. These desirable fruits are more than just personal characteristics of a pious person (if they are that at all). They are to be desired because they are products of our love for God and part of how God works to restore God's creation in Christ. If we learn to desire what God desires as part of authentic spirituality, and if we go about pursuing the desires of the Spirit as an aspect of spiritual formation, our lives will be rightly ordered by the love and purposes of God. This rightly ordered desire for God and for the good of others brings together spirituality and morality expressed in love of God and love of neighbor.

Disordered desires are exactly the opposite of the desires of the Spirit and take us away from the purposes of God's desire to restore relationships. The desires of the flesh are informed by the exaltation of one's self and utter disregard for God and God's creation. Like the fruit of the Spirit, the desires of the flesh are not just the personal character traits of an ungodly person. They are manifestations of disordered loves: a denial of God, an inordinate love of one's self, a disregarding lack of love for others. Paul names them in painful detail: "sexual immorality, impurity and debauchery; idolatry and witchcraft; hatred, discord, jealously, fits of rage, self-ambition, dissensions, factions and envy; drunkenness, orgies, and the like" (Gal 5:19–21). The warning is clear: "those who *live* like this will not inherent the Kingdom of God" (emphasis mine). Disordered desires cause further disorders in the world and contribute to the chaos caused by injustice, hatred, enmity, violence, immorality, greed, and abuse of God's creation. As Daniel Groody notes, "Without acknowledging God as the source and destiny of all human yearning, one easily frustrates the proper order of relationships, attempting to satisfy one's longing for the Creator with other gods, idols, people or possessions. Such a displacement inevitably leads to unhappiness, division, disorder and chaos . . ."[36] The effects of our disordered desires—on the lives of others and on creation, as well as on our own health and well-being—are devastating. They not only deny the source of ultimate desire—God—but they deny us participation in the kingdom of God, hence further separating and alienating us from the true source of life, with all of the dire impacts on other lives.

Implications for Christian Spirituality and Formation

Spirituality involves discerning and desiring what God desires. Spiritual formation is pursuing and patterning our lives to imbibe and embody these desires. Given that desires are central to formation, and that they are shaped and grounded in God, embodied in Jesus' life, and fostered by the gift of the Holy Spirit, what might be the implications for understanding the content and direction of Christian spirituality and for entering into a process of spiritual formation? Allow me to lift up three interrelated implications for our consideration. First, spirituality involves a freedom to focus on the good of others. Second, spirituality entails dispositions and actions. Third, spirituality is embodied, identifiable, and corporate.

Freedom to Focus on the Good of Others

In Galatians, Paul exhorts believers to use freedom rightly and for the purposes of fulfilling the command to love our neighbor as ourselves (5:14). In light of the contrasts that frame Paul's arguments and exhortations in Galatians, freedom is set in opposition to slavery. In its immediate context in Galatians 5, Paul is referencing freedom from the Law, which would have required circumcision and moral rectitude in fulfilling the requirements of the Law. This Christ has done so freedom takes the direction of freedom to serve and to love others as fulfillment of the law of Christ. By moving on to the command to "live by the Spirit," Paul is implying that there is now a choice before the Galatian Christians, and hence before us, to determine how to use our freedom given what Christ has done. Will our freedom be a form of license, a type of unhinged and independent freedom to pursue our

---

36. Groody, *Globalization, Spirituality, and Justice*, 67. See also the important book by Peters, *Sin*, for a helpful analysis of the social dimensions and impacts of the seven deadly sins.

own course and indulge in the desires of our flesh? Or will it be a freedom marked by the desires of the Spirit that is bound to the good of others, of God and God's creation? Freedom can be used to indulge one's sinful nature or used to serve others in love (5:13). To be free means not just liberty but to be unenslaved. One might be free in some sense of independence and liberation yet still enslaved by the desires and pursuits associated with the sinful nature (5:19–21). At the heart of the contrast between freedom and enslavement, according to Barclay, lies a choice before us between these competing desires of the flesh and Spirit. The Galatians' freedom, and hence ours, is "not absolute, for their walk in the Spirit will set them against the flesh and thus define the moral choices they must make."[37] Freedom is guided and constrained by the choice before us: between the desires of the sinful nature and the desires and fruit of the Spirit.

This conflict between desires presses us to discern which ones to pursue and why. Freedom is not to be used for indulgence of our own desires but instead in pursuit of the desires of the Spirit, wherein our true freedom lies. This is freedom to love God and to make wise and responsible choices that will impact our lives and the lives of others. Here is the hope and direction that Paul provides for our discernment and pursuit of good desires so crucial for Christian spirituality and formation. It is contained in the command, "Walk by the Spirit" (Gal 5:16). The motif of walking is a prominent one from the Torah. In the Old Testament, *halak* (Hebrew, "to walk") signifies a way of life, decisions, commitments, and conduct guided by and in line with God's commands.[38] In the New Testament, this meaning is retained and finds its fuller connection with the life of Christ as "the way, the truth and the life" (John 14:6). To walk in the Spirit is to walk in the ways of Christ, what the Galatians would have "immediately recognize[d] as the *continuation* of the way they began their lives in Christ (5.1–5)."[39] It is Christ who offers freedom, and it is the kind of freedom that Christ offers that shifts the focus from ourselves to others. It is a freedom to be who God (re)created us to be in Christ, becoming more fully human by loving and serving God and others.

Richard Bauckham notes four significant features of freedom from a New Testament perspective, two of which have important connections for

---

37. Barclay, *Obeying the Truth*, 112. See also the rich essay "Freedom and Desire" by Farley.

38. Matera, *Galatians*, 206.

39. Barclay, *Obeying the Truth*, 111. Italics in original.

how we conceive of the relationships between freedom and spirituality. He writes, "Christian freedom, in the New Testament, is certainly not purely inward and individual, but concerns the outward, social relationships of Christians in the church."[40] It is important to remember the very social nature of the majority of Paul's epistles. They are written to churches and groups of Christians, addressing theological issues, common concerns, and ways of relating to and treating each other consistent with the gospel they have received and now live. Our common life is a concern to God, and we are shaped in our common life. The spiritual health of our communities has significant implications for the spiritual health of its members as well as implications for our witness to the world. To walk in the Spirit is not an interiorized, private endeavor that emphasizes one's relationship with God as the primary relationship to which to attend. Spirituality, walking and living by the Spirit, is essentially relational and is shaped and nurtured in relationship with God and others.

To walk in the Spirit is to fulfill the law of Christ by loving and serving others. Walking in the Spirit results in a focus on others, which is a manifestation of the fruit of the Spirit. This is a second feature of freedom in the New Testament, what Bauckham calls "freedom as voluntary service."[41] We are freed from the tyranny of fulfilling our own sinful desires and demanding that our needs be met, and now free to focus on others. When we fail to realize that our freedom in Christ is for others, and not for the pursuit of own desires, we live out a stunted spirituality, an "exaggerated and prolonged adolescence," according to Bauckham. He writes, "In the relentless pursuit of autonomy, at the cost of community and belonging, contemporary Western society is living out an exaggerated and prolonged adolescence. The isolation, the loneliness, and the emptiness are the prodigal's pig-swill. The fullest freedom is not to be found in being as free from others as possible, but in the freedom we give each other when we belong to each other in loving relationships."[42]

---

40. Bauckham, *God and the Crisis of Freedom*, 14. According to Bauckham, the four features of freedom in the New Testament are an expansion of liberation from oppression in the Old Testament to include liberation from all areas of human bondage; freedom from slavery to become a slave of Christ; freedom as voluntary service; and freedom to live in oppressive structures while working to transform them.

41. Ibid., 15.

42. Ibid., 18.

Christian spirituality is shaped, nurtured, and guided in the context of community, for the benefit of community.[43] These communities are the Trinity and the community of faith, which then spill out and into the entire world in joyful witness and loving, just service. Christian spirituality has its roots in the community of the Trinitarian God. As Edith Humphrey asserts, "Our spirituality, if it is truly Christian, must be Trinitarian-shaped."[44] Christian spirituality flows from a relationship with Father, Son, and Spirit as our lives are continuations of the new creation that God is bringing about in Christ through the work of the Holy Spirit. It is grounded in the love and care of God for all God created, modeled, and patterned after the life of Jesus, and empowered by the Holy Spirit as a source of energy, wisdom, guidance, and truth that now makes the Christian life possible. Christian spirituality is "ecstastic" in that it comes from outside ourselves, from God, and draws us outward to relationship with God and others.[45]

Allow me to imaginatively extend the contrast that Paul provides in Galatians between the desires of the sinful nature and the fruit of the Spirit to differences between Christian spirituality and a kind of "fleshly" spirituality that is focused on one's self. If spirituality is about discerning and pursuing right desires based on God's Trinitarian life, then a spirituality that is solely focused on the status and health of one's own spiritual life and does not attend to the needs of others is a disordered, one-sided spirituality. Humphrey reminds us that "all that is 'spiritual' is not holy."[46] This is why I started my discussion on Christian spirituality with an understanding of right desires and discernment, consideration of Scripture, and theological moorings. These give spirituality its distinct *Christian* shape, direction, and purpose, and guide our processes and patterns of formation. Without these, our spirituality is left to our own whims and aspirations. It becomes "fleshly" in the sense that it is overly inward and focused on

---

43. While I believe community is a normative context for the formation of Christian spirituality and morality, I do share a feminist critique of communities that demand uniformity as a condition of acceptance, and communities that collapse difference into a false sense of sameness. It matters the kinds of community we have in mind for the formation of whole and holy selves, since not all communities are whole and holy and committed to the flourishing of all persons, especially women. See Albrecht, *Character of Our Communities*.

44. Humphrey, *Ecstasy and Intimacy*, 84.

45. Ibid., 3. This is how Humphrey conceives of "ecstasy" (from the Greek, *ek-static*), which draws us outward into intimacy with the Trinity.

46. Ibid., 203.

ourselves and disconnected from the life of God, the concerns of Christ, and the illuminating work of the Spirit. It may be a false spirituality that is highly individualistic, relies on one's "inner self," is indiscriminate in picking and choosing from eclectic religious sources, and discounts and minimizes "faith seeking understanding" for clarity on the content of our faith and the scriptural and theological narratives that inform it.[47] A false spirituality tends to focus on "spiritual freedom" for the sake of freedom, not unlike libertarian conceptions of freedom for freedom's sake, and is empty of the communal dimensions and requisite responsibilities to attend to others. Christian spirituality has a specific shape and it serves specific purposes. Spiritual formation is not about self-discovery and improvement but about the shaping of desires, dispositions, and behavior. These are given a particular shape in the virtues that we know as the fruit of the Spirit.

Dispositions and Actions

The second implication for spiritual formation is the focus on both dispositions and actions. It is easy to appreciate and appropriate the traits or virtues that Paul describes as the "fruit of the Spirit" as inner qualities of personal piety. Except for a sociopath, who does not want to be more loving, more joyful, or more peaceful? Who does not want to be known as kind, good, and faithful? Why are gentle people and those who are moderate and self-controlled easier to be around? Yet these virtues that Paul describes are more than just inner dispositions and personal qualities. They are descriptions of a unified character that is visible to others. They make us integrated in being and doing, persons of integrity. These virtues make no sense unless there are ways of expressing and observing them—unless there is a context and set of relationships in which they are developed, formed, and practiced. Groody notes that spirituality is concerned with the "terrain of the heart," not in an overly interiorized and hidden sense, but "with what one values, with how one lives out one's relationships, and in particular with how one responds to the most vulnerable members of the human family."[48] Perhaps we are not the best judges of our growth in goodness, faithfulness, or gentleness. Perhaps others are best able to see our spiritual growth given that they are recipients of our love, faithfulness, kindness, and goodness (or lack thereof). These fruit point to the reality of dialogical relationships between

47. Ibid., 203–12.
48. Groody, *Globalization, Spirituality, and Justice*, 11.

our character—or who we are and who we are becoming—and our actions. We are what we do and we do what we are, to various degrees. Christian spirituality and formation is about who we are *and* what we do. Christian spirituality and spiritual growth have important social dimensions in that they are observable and fruitful for the lives of others.

This is important for understanding the kind of visible, public spirituality depicted in the fruit of the Spirit in Galatians 5:22–26 that involves both dispositions and behavior. The divide between "inward," with its focus on the interior life, and "outward," with a consequential emphasis on what results from one's interior growth, is unhealthy in my view and functionally detrimental to a wholistic conception of spirituality and formation. Given the already individualistic thrust of many conceptions of spirituality that have been appropriated by Christians, the danger of prioritizing spirituality as *primarily* inward and *secondarily* outward misses the very communal dimensions of the fruits of the Spirit as they connect dispositions with behavior in ways that are visible and public. As Gordon Fee observes, ". . . from beginning to end the concern [of Galatians 5:13—6:10] is with *Christian life in community,* not with an interior life of the individual believer."[49] Christian life in community must concern itself with how we treat others as a matter of genuine spirituality. If we understand the fruit of the Spirit as akin to virtues, which I will discuss in greater detail in the next chapter, spiritual formation must involve not just the growth in dispositions and affections but, in tandem, the growth in habitual behaviors coherent with what we believe.

For spirituality to be authentic, it must not be "confined to an individual's 'care of the soul,' since its practices and frame of reference are communally based and oriented to action with and for others."[50] What is behind Paul's admonition to "live by the Spirit" and "walk by the Spirit" is something far more complex and important than just developing inner dispositions of love, joy, peace, patience, kindness, generosity, faithfulness, gentleness, and self-control. We do not become more loving and *then* love; we do not become more patient and *then* exercise patience with others; and we do not become more faithful and *then* remain faithful in relationships. Since spiritual formation involves pursuit and practice, it is probable that in our practicing of love, we become more loving; in our practicing of patience, we become more patient; and in our practicing of faith, we become

49. Fee, *Galatians*, 202. Italics in original.

50. Spohn, *Go and Do Likewise*, 36.

more faithful. Somehow, even in the doing, by "walking by the Spirit," we are formed and our desires are shaped according to God's desires for our lives. This is the kind of integration between spirituality and morality that is important, where God's deepest desires become ours and our desires to express God's desires are manifest in how we love and live with others.

Embodied, Identifiable, and Corporate Spirituality

I have been arguing that an individualistic spirituality is oxymoronic based on my reflections on Galatians 5. A spirituality that stresses and privileges an interior life makes little sense according to Scripture and in light of God's desires for God's creation, the life of Christ, and the work of the Holy Spirit. This Trinitarian-shaped life is now taken on by the people of God, who have been set free to walk in the ways of Jesus and in the Spirit, to discern, pursue, and practice the desires of God. Hence the third implication for spirituality that relates to the first two: spirituality is embodied, identifiable, and corporate.

The aim of Paul's exhortation is to create a moral ethos grounded in the work of the Spirit that is to characterize this community of Christian believers so that their identity is formed together. This makes Christian identity corporate. We are to be identified with Christ and recognized by the norms of the fruit of the Spirit, walking in the ways of the Spirit as Christ walked. This new spirituality reality should produce new moral horizons and ethical commitments. These norms guide the community in their relationships with others in the community and those outside the community. The fruit of the Spirit establishes a pattern of life incumbent on all who claim membership. New expectations are established for behavior and proper ways of responding to and relating to others.[51] Even as standards of behavior depicted by the fruit of the Spirit are expected, so too is forgiveness a group norm when we inevitably fail to fulfill these expectations. This also identifies a group as "in Christ" when not just the fruit of the Spirit becomes normative but so does forgiveness and the ongoing offer of hope as we continually "provoke one another to love and good deeds" (Heb 10:24).

51. See the following two articles on social identity theory and Scripture: Esler, "Social Identity, the Virtues, and the Good Life," and Ukwuegbu, "Paraenesis, Identity-Defining Norms, or Both?"

Christian spirituality is corporate, embodied, and identifiable. As corporate, it is formed and lived out in the context of Christian faith, guided by Scripture and rooted in the practices of Christian communities. Spirituality is embodied. It is not the denial of our bodies but the reshaping of the desires of our "flesh" so that we live more rightly and justly *in* our bodies. Christian spirituality is identifiable and visible. It is open to questioning, judgment, and correction. It is distinct from more "fleshly" forms of spirituality that privilege one's self and are individualistic and hidden from view. The distinct identity of Christian spirituality is important given the plethora of spiritualities that attract us today both in and outside of the church. As Alan Padgett reminds us,

> The plain fact is that Christ has called us into community, and so life in the Spirit of Christ is a spiritual life in community. New Age spirituality is eclectic, private, and individualistic. Biblical spirituality grounded in the gospel and the Holy Spirit is communal, traditional, and practical. The fruit of the Spirit is exactly those virtues that tend to build up community: love, joy, peace, patience, kindness, goodness, faith, meekness, and self-control. Paul is writing against a group of leaders in the Galatian churches who thought they were "spiritual" but whose conduct showed them to be far from Christ.[52]

Conclusion

I covered quite a bit of terrain in this chapter. It was important to provide some degree of diagnosis to address the questions, How did we get here? and, Where are we? We are at a place of heightened fascination with spirituality, and a spirituality that makes no demands on us is certainly appealing. We might be more interested in spirituality but less concerned with being spiritually formed in light of God's desires—and therefore, what we should desire. I pressed these points because of the tendency I have observed in my own contexts for a kind of gnostic spirituality that is dualistic, hidden from public view, overly interior, makes claims to superiority and super-spirituality, and is overly experiential. By reorienting spirituality based on Scripture and theological considerations, my hope is to ground spirituality in right desires, in both pursuit and practice of these right desires that encompass affections and behaviors. Spirituality is embodied, identifiable,

52. Padgett, "Walk in the Spirit," 344.

and corporate, and it frees us to focus on the good of others in loving service. Why? Because this is what God desires, what Jesus has done, and because the Holy Spirit draws us outward and empowers us to pursue and practice the fruit of the Spirit.

In my exploration and use of Galatians 5, it has been hard to maintain a boundary between spirituality and morality. It has been hard to do because it *is* hard to do, given the interrelationship between them in Scripture and Christian faith. I will explore the contours of Christian moral formation in the next chapter, where again the boundaries between spirituality and morality will be difficult to retain. But this is a good thing since our desire for God spills over into understanding the right things to desire, which is the focus of the next chapter.

two

Right Things to Desire

STATISTICS CAN BE TELLING and depressing. This was the case when I read a Barna Group survey from September 2010.[1] The survey asked participants what differences and changes they experienced in their lives over the last five years as a result of their Christian faith. What is revealing about this survey is that it asked about evidentiary changes in practices of faith and religious activities, not necessarily changes in belief, save for a few select topics. Here is a snapshot of the results. "Among the adults randomly sampled for the nationwide survey, just 7 percent said they could think of any religious beliefs, practices, or preferences they had altered during the past five years." Of these 7 percent, "about one-third of adults who experienced any change at all mentioned an increase in some aspect of their faith commitment. Fourteen percent said they had stepped up their commitment to the Christian faith, in general; 12 percent cited an increase in their religious activity; and 9 percent indicated their commitment to God had grown."

George Barna offered analyses on the causes of these trends. Since the survey respondents were adults, Barna reaffirms that many churchgoers have already established their faith and related practices much earlier in their lives; therefore habits of religious practice may be more difficult to shape in those who come to faith later in life. Barna also notes that this pattern may reflect the ineffectiveness of adult discipleship programs in churches. Second, Barna suggests that the lack of relationship between faith and practice may be related to the disinterest or ineffectiveness of church leaders in assisting people to make connections between their faith and the real-life, complex issues of our world today. People are not provoked to think very deeply about the implications of their faith for how they

1. Barna Group, "Survey Finds Lots of Spiritual Dialogue but Not Much Change."

deliberate and respond to social ethical issues. Third, the changes that the Barna Group survey did note were changes in emotions and devotion that were described as spiritual, whereas the least amount of change was in the integration of faith into all dimensions of a person's life. Finally, while the majority said that their religious faith was important enough to them to share with others, the substance of what they share is thin. Receiving comfort and a sense of personal well-being from faith was shared but not much else. So while this may be helpful to those needing the words of comfort that faith provides, it further reinforces the perception that Christian faith has little to say or contribute to the hard questions and troubling moral issues that we face.

Drawing on the insights from the previous chapter on trends in spirituality may help explain some of Barna's findings. Spirituality is perceived as otherworldly, related to some higher plane of existence, relegated to a personal space, and cut off from the rough-and-tumble terrain of real life. It may be viewed as an inner state of well-being, not necessarily something that is formed and practiced in the context of faith communities, let alone in the "real world." Its scope of interest is narrow and often does not include the very concrete dimensions of human life and social dimensions of Christian faith that involve hard questions, troubling ethical issues, and concrete practices.

Perhaps at its most basic level, the Barna Group survey reveals the disjunction between spirituality and morality that is the concern I am addressing in this book. In light of the trends Barna discovered, which many of us may have experienced in our own church contexts, my aim is to integrate Christian spirituality and morality as normative for Christian faith and practice. Spirituality is about our ultimate desires, primarily our desire for God, and how this desire gives shape, direction, and substance to our lives through processes of spiritual formation as we learn to discern, desire, and pursue the right things. Christian spirituality is located in a relationship with the Trinitarian God, directed by Scripture, focused outward on God and others, and formed and lived out in community.

Morality is also about desires. It is about the right things to desire, and the shaping and embodying of these desires. It is how and why we make moral judgments based on our understanding of the goodness of God and what God desires, and how this informs how we actually live and the ethical choices we make. Like spirituality, morality is grounded in God and deals with our deepest desires, which makes the link between spiritual and moral formation explicit. In this chapter, I will probe the shape and direction of Christian morality by first offering a crash course in Christian ethics in order to name my assumptions and methodological considerations. As in the previous chapter, I will offer theological reflection on a text of Scripture that narrates what God desires. I will work with the three interrelated aspects of Christian spirituality I introduced in the last chapter in a parallel fashion, revisiting them and expanding them given the dimensions of Christian morality. The parallels are the capacity to care justly for others, the development and practice of social virtues, and becoming wise moral actors in corporate contexts.

Crash Course in Christian Ethics

Since this book is not primarily about Christian ethics, it's important to name some of my assumptions about the content, scope, sources, and methods of Christian ethical reflection and morality; these assumptions undergird my explorations and proposals in this chapter. My first assumption is that the Christian ethical life is not separate from our ongoing growth as disciples of Jesus Christ. Learning to follow Jesus in practices of obedience is part of our moral growth in taking on the concerns of Christ. The dichotomy between the life of discipleship and Christian ethics is not only false but dangerous for the ways in which it truncates the wholistic and demanding nature of the gospel. While Christian ethics must involve thoughtful and careful use of Scripture, tradition, reason, and experience in making moral judgments, it starts with the important claim that patterning our lives after Christ must involve particular ways of seeing the world and responding in the ways in which Christ might respond.[2] We are called to follow Christ in all dimensions of life if we truly believe that Christ is Lord.

My second assumption is that the Christian ethical life is dynamic, not static, and embodied in a way of life, not solely in absolutist kinds of principles as the sum total of our moral obligations. Christian ethics concerns who we are and who we are becoming as much as the decisions and commitments we make. These must work in tandem: our character matters and so do our decisions. Our decisions shape our character, and our character

---

2. The recovery of the centrality of Christ in Christian ethics has been important and is represented in the following works: Burridge, *Imitating Jesus*; Harrington and Keenan, *Jesus and Virtue Ethics*; Spohn, *Go and Do Likewise*; Stassen and Gushee, *Kingdom Ethics*; Verhey, *Remembering Jesus*; and Yoder, *Politics of Jesus*.

informs our decisions.[3] This is an important aspect of virtue ethics that has received renewed attention in Christian moral thought. Virtue ethics is an important corrective to the tendency to limit Christian ethical reflection to *just* decisions and positions on "hard" issues. Virtue ethics places emphasis on character formation and makes stronger connections between who we are and how we live. It posits that we are formed by what we love and desire. What we love and desire must have some ultimate point of reference, a moral vision, if you will, of goodness and ultimate purposes for human life. For Christians, it is God and God's good purposes for human life that orient us. Desires or affections, dispositions, and habits are key components of virtue ethics and for moral formation, as they are for Christian spirituality. They are shaped over a lifetime and continually oriented and reoriented by ultimate desires and goods. Habits are the means by which we practice becoming more virtuous. Habits enable goods and desires to become incarnated and impactful for the good of others. They are not just for our own moral formation. They are forms of goodness extended outward to others for their good and flourishing.

While I appreciate the emphasis on character and virtue as crucial for Christian ethics, I do not want to juxtapose them with or privilege them over the hard and sometimes agonizing responsibility of making moral judgments about complex issues, as if assuming who we are is more important than what we do. Both are important for Christian ethics. Being and doing must be kept together, resisting the danger to privilege one over the other. We must decide and act out of our sense of what is good, right, fitting, just, and true, and the resources of our conscience and character. Often these choices are difficult. Instead of pursuing the right decision, often we are left with the best or better decision, or the least bad option out of a bunch of crummy ones. We need resources to make these difficult choices that often extend beyond our own moral capacities and even our character. Just as we become disciples by learning to follow Christ, so we constantly learn and explore the moral dimensions of our faith as we confront various issues over the course of our lives, seeking wisdom from God, our Christian communities, and others. None of us arrive at moral perfection. However, given the dynamic nature of moral formation, building "moral competencies" and growing in wisdom are important, and we must commit to do these over a lifetime, recognizing that the Christian ethical

3. See the helpful book by Connors and McCormick, *Character, Choices and Community*.

life encompasses who we are, how we live, what we love and desire, and the choices and commitments we make.[4]

My third assumption is that the sources we use as Christians to make moral assessments and ethical judgments must be used with care and integrity. This is especially true when it comes to how we use Scripture to engage in ethical deliberation and in making moral judgments. While most Christian ethicists affirm the Bible as a primary source in ethics, the weight that it bears and how we go about using Scripture are different matters. This is an issue of methodology that extends beyond the limits of this book but, nonetheless, is important to address, albeit briefly.[5] Scripture provides a rich, complex, and important narrative framework for the Christian moral life by shaping moral vision, grounding duties and obligations, and forming our character. Scripture offers us God's moral vision for human life and creation, bookended by God's creative intentions for *shalom* in Genesis 1 and 2 and the complete, just, and life-giving restoration of God's creation encompassed in the visions of Revelation. The Christian moral life takes shape informed by these pictures of what should have been and what will be, which guide the "oughtness" of our lives: how we ought to be, how we ought to live, what we ought to do, and why.

Scripture elucidates our duties and obligations to God and others. These duties and obligations are not abstract principles but are instructions for patterned ways of obedient living based on God's covenant loyalty to us and our covenant obligations to God and others. While Scripture contains rules and principles, it cannot be reduced to a book of rules and principles; this would be to ignore the narrative context that gives shape and meaning to the didactic portions of Scripture, as well as its other genres. Seeing Scripture simply as a rulebook diminishes its role in ethics and moral formation.[6] Using Scripture in this way tends to reduce the moral life to "just obeying the right rules," even when rules themselves might be morally problematic and acontextual. Behind the commands and prohibitions of Scripture are larger narrative concerns deeply connected with the vision for human life God offers in Scripture. Obedience to Scripture is a crucial part of Christian moral formation, but it is not obedience for the sake of obedience, particularly if it is motivated by fear of punishment and hope

---

4. For a description of moral competency, see Selznick, *Moral Commonwealth*, 33–38.

5. See two important works on Scripture and ethics: Birch and Rasmussen, *Bible and Ethics in the Christian Life*, and Spohn, *What Are They Saying about Scripture and Ethics?*

6. See Corbin Reuschling, "Trust and Obey," 59–77.

of reward. It is an obedience, according to Emilie Townes, that "is always related to justice. It is requested of people directly concerned with shaping the world entrusted to human beings. Obedience implies responsibility: a decision to first discover God's will and then decide what must be done.... Jesus requires an obedience that has its eyes wide open as we accept responsibility for the order of the world and engage in transforming that order."[7]

Along with providing orienting moral vision and grounding our ethical obligations in Scripture's narrative direction, the Bible also prods us to consider the "not yet" dimensions and always growing nature of our character. There is an ongoing feature to our character formation that Scripture addresses as "working out our salvation" (Phil 2:12–13), "pressing on toward" completeness in Christ (Phil 3:12–14), making "every effort to add to our faith" (2 Pet 1:5–8), and living as beloved children of God even as "what we will be has not yet been made known" (1 John 3:1–3). Who we are matters to God, as does who we are becoming. Scripture offers us avenues of important self-reflection on who we are and who we are called to become. Word and Spirit cooperate in the continuous formation of our selves, forming us more and more into the likeness of Christ through such habits and disciplines as prayer, giving, worship, service, hospitality, Sabbath keeping, doing justice, showing mercy, and loving others. While these are givens—normative standards, if you will—of Christian faith and practice, they are not automatic. While Word and Spirit are gifts of God crucial for formation, so is our willingness to hear, respond, and receive who Word and Spirit are calling us to be, become, and do. Character formation in Christian ethics is not a navel-gazing experiment of self-discovery but instead an honest and sober assessment *of* ourselves over the course of our lives; it involves the continual examination of our desires, affections, and actions in light of God's affections, desires, and actions.

My final assumption is that the Christian moral life is grounded in the Trinity.[8] Intimations of this are in my first three assumptions, but I make it more explicit here. God is the source of all that is good and morally excellent (2 Pet 1:3–10). Jesus is the ideal human and "the visible expression of the invisible God" (Col 1:15) whose life is normative for us. The Holy Spirit provides us with the power to pursue and act on what is good. These divine Trinitarian relationships ground our own lives and provide the communal

---

7. Townes, "Living in the New Jerusalem," 88.

8. See my chapter, "Being and Becoming," in *Becoming Whole and Holy*, by Brown, Dahl, and Corbin Reuschling.

context for the shaping of our character, and for understanding how God acts in and on behalf of the world to restore justice and right relationships. This makes Christian ethics deeply theological and inherently social.

By now I hope the relationships between spirituality and morality are coming into sharper focus. They flow from a relationship with God, and therefore have close connections with God's own desires, affections, and actions in the world. Spirituality and morality are concrete and embodied, not abstractions that occur outside the material nature of human life. They cannot be codified in ungrounded principles and abstracted from real lives and real communities. Instead, spirituality and morality inform how we live. They are guided by Scripture. They have a narrative context and content that orients the processes of spiritual and moral formation toward desired ends. Spirituality and morality both require making normative judgments about what is good and desirable. Spiritual formation is about desiring the right things. Morality must be oriented by the right things to desire, the topic to which I now turn.

Right Things to Desire

If spirituality involves discerning and desiring right things, which for Christians is our desire for God, then morality requires discernment about the right things to desire. God desires relationships with God's creation. But for these relationships to truly reflect what God desires, they must be marked with justice, righteousness, and mercy.

Even a cursory reading of the prophetic material in the Scriptures gives us a glimpse of the importance of justice for people who claim to belong to God. The demand to "do justice" is woven through the worship, piety, and covenant responsibilities of the people of God. There was to be no separation between religious observances and moral obligations in covenantal faith. As Cain Hope Felder writes, "*The vertical piety of the cult that praises and acknowledges the sovereignty of God has a horizontal parallel specifying the believers' social obligations to others*."[9] The relationships between loyalty to the one true God and obligations to others were inherent in the law and covenantal responsibilities that specify both religious observances and ways of treating others. Belief and practice go hand in hand. One's piety is not separate from one's commitment to justice and social responsibility.

9. Felder, *Troubling Biblical Waters*, 60. Italics in original.

The peril of separating religious practice and social obligations, particularly related to justice, comes under sharp critique by the prophets in the Hebrew Bible. So while there was no shortage of devotional practices among the people of God, there was a dearth of attention to matters of justice, care for the needy, and the use of material resources, while abuse of political and religious power and oppressive practices became prevalent. The prophets were not shy about expressing the danger of the dichotomy between piety—one they deemed to be false—and matters of justice. An integral part of true worship of God was attention to justice and mercy. The prophets' admonitions are vast and their words indicting for those who neglect what God desires, what God deems as good, and what God considers as true and acceptable worship. The prophet Micah speaks for God with clarity:

> He has shown you, O mortal, what is good.
> And what does the Lord require of you?
> To act justly and to love mercy
> and to walk humbly with your God. (Mic 6:8)

This eighth-century prophet was addressing concerns about the faithfulness, moral ethos, and spiritual credibility of God's people at a particular point in their history. The sweep of the Old Testament narrative involves God's creation and covenant, the calling of Abram to make a new people, a nation to be a blessing, and the eventual enslavement in Egypt and subsequent liberation of Israel by God.[10] This wilderness community had no god but God to protect them from the powerful nations that surrounded them. Through the prophet Moses, the law is given as a grace and gift to guide God's people and to mark their religious practices and community life as different from those of other nations. They live "in exodus" but always in hope of reaching the land promised to them, eventually arriving through dubious means of conquest and conflict to take up residence.[11] This offers God's people a new kind of reality: a place, power, and political

10. I imagine some of my colleagues in Hebrew Bible are wincing at this simple reduction of the complexities and multiplicities of narratives, literary genres, historical span, and diversity of the Old Testament material into a somewhat pithy metanarrative. I'm not proposing a reductionistic grand metanarrative but instead simply want to understand how and where to locate Micah's concerns. For important overviews of Old Testament narrative and ethics, see Birch, *Let Justice Roll Down*, and Wright, *Old Testament Ethics for the People of God*.

11. See the recent work by my colleague and friend Dan Hawk, *Joshua in 3-D*.

organization. Upon being granted kings of all sorts, Israel expands its economic, military, and political power. With this move from the margins to the center, something happens to the spiritual and moral sensibilities of God's people. While their religious apparatus is developed and perhaps more sophisticated, fundamental covenant responsibilities of loyalty and devotion to God and care for others are neglected and forgotten, even by some priests and prophets. They are smug in their self-righteousness, confident that God remains on their side regardless of how they act.

It is this context and historical moment into which the prophet Micah speaks, at the peak of Israel's political power, vast economic resources, military might, and religiosity. Micah, likely a professional prophet, stands in the line of Israel's prophets who are passionately driven by and charged with the need to speak for God to the people.[12] This prophetic speaking involved truth telling about current conditions and their causes, an appeal to change and repentance, reminders of covenant loyalty and responsibility, and offerings of hope. Micah's context was religious yet morally bankrupt. It's important to note that it was not covenant faith and the sacrificial system that was the problem and the object of Micah's prophetic critique. It was the failure of God's people to discern, desire, and decide to do the things that God requires, namely, justice. While God's people wanted to lay blame on God for imminent disasters from foreign invaders or feign ignorance about the causes of their suffering, Micah reminds them that their actions have brought about their current crises, in particular their neglect of justice, mercy, and covenant loyalty. Dishonest economic and political practices, abuse of power, oppression of the poor by the wealthy, exploitative prophets preaching for profit, and violence and legitimized wickedness—these and other unjust practices were prevalent among the people.

Micah speaks into this situation on behalf of God in the form of a trial (1:2). God has charges to level against God's people and a case against those who make claims to be "spiritually right" with God yet who willfully and blatantly violate moral requirements inherent in their faith.[13] What were these charges? The list of divine grievances is a long one: plotting evil and harm of others (2:1); coveting and seizing the properties of others (2:2);

---

12. I am drawing on the following sources for understanding the sociohistorical and literary context, purpose, and structure of the book of Micah: Baker, Alexander, and Waltke, *Obadiah, Jonah, and Micah*; Birch, *Let Justice Roll Down*; Carroll, "He Has Told You What is Good"; Heschel, *Prophets*; Jacobs, "Book of Micah"; Sweeney, *Twelve Prophets*; and Weinfeld, *Social Justice in Ancient Israel and in the Ancient Near East*.

13. See Corbin Reuschling, *Reviving Evangelical Ethics*, 134–36.

violence against innocents (2:8–9); abusive and violent power (3:1–3); preaching for profit (3:5–7); abhorring justice and perverting equity (3:9); misuse of the Lord's name (3:11); cheating and dishonesty (6:10–12); and corrupt business and legal practices that exploit others (6:12–14). While it is easy to see these oracles as prophesies of doom, and rightly so, Micah also offered ways forward for those who hear and receive these hard words. Repentance and return to covenant loyalty and obligations were responses called for as agreements to the charges that God brings. With repentance and obedience comes hope.

In chapter 6, Micah presents the Lord's case. The Lord is both defendant, given our propensity to blame God for our ills, and litigant before the accused. The Lord has stated the "controversy with Israel" (6:2) as litigant, the one who has been offended, while also offering a defense (6:3–5) as a testimony of God's goodness and saving acts. This brings us to the section central for discerning what God desires from people, informing our commitment to the right things as key for Christian ethics. According to Martin Sweeney, verses six through eight in Micah 6 may have possibly been a "generic form of the Temple entrance liturgy."[14] Worshippers may have asked these four rhetorical questions:

> With what shall I come before the Lord, and bow myself before God on high?
>
> Shall I come before him with burnt offerings, with calves a year old?
>
> Will the Lord be pleased with thousands of rams, with ten thousands of rivers of oil?
>
> Shall I give my firstborn for my transgression, the fruit of my body for the sin of my soul? (Mic 6:6–7)

Rhetorical questions have obvious answers that were likely evident to the hearers of these words in the context of worship: "He has told you, O mortal, what is good, and what does the Lord require of you but to do justice, and to love kindness, and to walk humbly with your God" (6:8). The requirements, even conditions of acceptable and true worship of God, involve doing justice, loving kindness, and walking humbly with God. These requirements flow right from God's own character and commitments: God is just and God has been loyal, kind, and faithful. Walking with

---

14. Sweeney, *Twelve Prophets*, 398.

humility recognizes our dependence on and gratitude for God's justice and faithfulness.

What does the Lord desire? The Lord requires the doing of justice. What is the nature of this kind of justice, which is so central to the true worship of God? Justice, or *mišpat*, is adherence to the law, and doing what is right as required by the law with its focus on cultic practices *and* moral responsibilities inherent to faith. In Scripture, this conception of justice is often linked with the word *tsedaqah*, usually translated as "righteousness." Birch notes the relationships between these terms in the following way: "Justice (*mišpat*) relates to the claim to life and participation by all persons in the structures and dealings of the community, and especially to equity in the legal system. Righteousness (*ṣedaqah*), a more personal term, refers to the expectations in relationship for intentions and actions that make for wholeness in that relationship."[15]

Justice in the Scriptures is not the ideological kind of justice so common in much of our current sociopolitical discourse. Justice cannot be reduced to ideas such as distribution, fairness, retribution, reward, rights, and equality. While these may be aspects of justice, they are not equivalent to the kind of justice called for in the Scriptures, where the qualities of justice and righteousness "are rooted in the character of God who *acted* in justice and righteousness toward the people. God then expects these qualities to be reflected in the life of God's people, in their relationships to one another and to God."[16] The justice we are to *do* is informed by God's intention for creation that our relationships be marked, guided, and structured by God's concern for the good of all creation. Justice involves making things right, naming evil, restoring what has been broken and lost—restoring persons and communities to wholeness marked by *shalom*, the rich biblical image of harmonious wholeness and right relations. The biblical concept of justice is relational and social in that it encompasses and concerns all that God created. Justice applies to each individual, to communities, to social structures and institutions, so that each might mediate the goods and benefits that God intends and those necessary for human life. Justice pays particular attention to those who are oppressed, powerless, and marginalized, placed on the fringes, away from the goods of society.

Along with doing justice, the Lord requires kindness and mercy. These words are translated from the theologically rich word *hesed*, the grand

---

15. Birch, *Let Justice Roll Down*, 259–60.

16. Ibid., 260. Emphasis mine.

biblical notion of loyalty and faithfulness. Hearers of these words might quickly hearken back to the covenant, which was to structure their lives together as God's people. God has been faithfully loyal to God's people in spite of what we have deserved. In turn, we are called to be loyal to God and faithful in fulfilling the obligations incumbent upon us as recipients of God's kindness and mercy. We are to show kindness, love, and mercy to others. We are to be loyal to God and faithful in expressing the things that God desires. As an expression of loyalty to God, one was to be kind and faithful in their dealing with others. The lack of faithfulness in such matters as economics, acquisition of property and wealth, exploitation of those on the margins, and abuse of legal and political systems came under the indictment of the prophets as violations of the requirements of kindness, loyalty, and justice. As God has been kind, loyal, and just, so should we in all matters of social life.

The Lord also requires that we walk humbly with God, in grateful dependence that we have experienced God's justice, mercy, and faithfulness. According to Sweeney, this sense of humility is akin to wisdom, in contrast to those who are proud and arrogant, who have no need of God and are convinced they have all of the answers necessary for right living.[17] Walking with God adds an important practical dimension to accompanying commands to do justice and to love mercy and kindness. Wisdom is not the accumulation of knowledge *about* God but, instead, is a practiced way of life that understands what God asks of us and *how* to put into practice what God desires and requires. Wisdom is more often related to our conduct as the ability to apply what we know to how we should live. Ellen Davis writes that "wisdom denotes a way of thinking—and equally, of living— that brings us into enduring harmony with family, with neighbors near and far, with our physical environment and ultimately, with the whole created order."[18] As the Scriptures affirm, learning wisdom is necessary for "wise dealing, righteousness, justice, and equity" and for fairness, prudence, and skills for living (Ps 111:10; Prov 1:2–6). This process of growing in wisdom requires humility and the awesome reverence of God as the beginning of all knowledge and right ways of living (Prov 1:7).

It's important to note that the prophetic critique was not directed toward religious practices *per se* but towards the absence and neglect of justice that was a requirement for true worship. As Heschel writes, "Of

17. Sweeney, *Twelve Prophets*, 400.
18. Davis, "Surprised by Wisdom," 267.

course, the prophets did not condemn the practice of sacrifice in itself. . . . They did, however, claim that deeds of injustice vitiate both sacrifice and prayer. Men [*sic*] may not drown out the cries of the oppressed with the noises of humans, nor buy off the Lord with increased offerings. The prophets disparaged the cult when it became a substitute for righteousness. It is precisely the implied recognition of the value of the cult that lends force to their insistence that there is something far more precious than sacrifice."[19]

There was no shortage of religious and pious practices. It was a shortage of and disregard for justice that aroused the ire of the prophets. There is an intricate and integrated relationship between the worship of God and our moral obligations to "do justice" to the point that the prophets indict forms of worship as false, fetid, and unfaithful that disregard social obligations to others. The prophets assume this relationship between faith in God, worship, and the requirement to "do justice" to be a given, one for which they need not apologize. The prophets' case, and hence God's, was not to convince people that justice was a requirement of faith. It was assumed to be a requirement of faith based on loyalty to God. Wolterstorff observes: "The prophets and the psalmist do not argue the case that alleviating the plight of the lowly is required by justice. They assume it. When they speak of God's justice, when they enjoin their hearers to practice justice, when they complain to God about the absence of justice, they take for granted that justice requires alleviating the plight of the lowly. They save their breath for urging their readers to actually *practice* justice to the quartet of the vulnerable low ones."[20]

Wolterstorff also notes that the relationship between worship and justice is not to be conceived as worship *and* justice, or worship *then* justice, but as "*not* authentic liturgy *unless* justice."[21] In the prophets, worship is judged as inauthentic and vapid, a parody, *unless* there is justice, measured by attention to and concern for those most vulnerable to the injustices of society. Without attention to the needs of others, without an active struggle against injustices that destroy God's intentions for creation, and without a desire for the things that God desires, our worship practices come under

---

19. Heschel, *Prophets*, 196.

20. Wolterstorff, *Justice*, 76. The "quartet of the vulnerable ones" are widows, orphans, resident aliens, and the poor.

21. Wolterstorff, "Justice as a Condition of Authentic Liturgy," in *Hearing the Call*, 47. Italics in original.

a prophetic indictment because of the dichotomies we create between our spirituality and ethics, and our piety and practices. Wolterstorff goes on:

> It is, then, no mystery why Micah represented God as calling for justice in response to God's saving acts instead of calling for something quite different. God saves for shalom, for life abundant. And there is no life abundant without the people's justice. The significance of the covenant is that God and the people have jointly pledged to travel together on the road to human flourishing—God blessing, the people exhibiting wisdom, righteousness, justice, love, and mercy. The biblical critique of humankind is that we live with the illusion that we can get the blessing without the ethic and that the blessing will be enough for the flourishing—believing, in turn, that the way to secure the blessing without the ethic is to engage in the actions of the cult.[22]

The worship of God and doing justice go hand in hand. Worship is not authentic unless there is justice and unless we are committed to the struggle against injustice. It is in and through worship that we learn and are formed by what God desires, which should become the right things we must desire. The worship of God is not a "spiritual matter" concerned with achieving some kind of "ecstatic" experience that takes us away from the trials and tribulations of the world, that enables us to retreat to private spaces and enclaves. Worship draws us out toward God and others. In worship we are *reminded* of who God is, what God has done and is doing in fulfilling God's intentions for creation, and what God requires of us as faithful participants in this redemptive work. Justice is also not just an ethical matter, left to be guided by abstract principles that have little to do with Christian faith. The love of God grounds and guides our commitment to justice. What God loves, we should love. What God desires, we should desire. What God does, we should imitate within the limits of our creaturely existence as humans created in the Divine Image. God loves and desires justice, and so should we. As David Rensberger eloquently writes:

> When love has its proper place at the Christian center, it would require a painstaking effort to distinguish, let alone choose, between spirituality and social justice—and none at all to see and inhabit their unity. The Christian life is one life, one simple and complex, plain and mysterious, active and contemplative life. . . . [E]ach of us is also a piece of the wholeness of the Christian reality, and each of us has that wholeness available to be a guiding vision of what

22. Ibid., 51.

the integrated human life lived in relationship with God should be. Worship, peacemaking, evangelism, care for the earth, discipleship, prayer, and the quest for justice are all one thing, one single and beautifully multifaceted acting out of our love for God.[23]

Expressions of our love for God embodied in the joyful and persevering pursuit of what God desires, making them our own, shapes Christian spirituality and morality. Worship is morally forming when we are reminded again and again of what God desires. Practicing justice is spiritually forming since by it we pursue and embody what God desires. God has shown us what is good, and what God desires: to do justice, love kindness, and walk humbly with God. Like spirituality, morality is found in and flows from our desire for what God desires, creating an unbreakable link between Christian spirituality and morality.

Implications for Christian Morality and Formation

The implications of our desire for the right things as what guides and grounds Christian morality parallel the interrelated implications I offered in the previous chapter on Christian spiritual formation. God's desires give shape, direction, and content to moral formation where the practicing of justice out of love for God and others directs us toward the good of others, toward the practice and formation of social virtues, and toward heightening our moral sensibilities as actors in social contexts. These implications are also interrelated and spill over into each other as their connections with spiritual formation become more evident.

Caring for the Good of Others

Like spiritual formation, which involves the freedom to focus on others, moral formation involves developing capacities and commitments to care for the good of others. Before exploring in more detail what this involves and how moral capacities for it are formed, it's important to clarify what I mean by the "good of others." I stand in a trajectory of moral theologians who locate the source of goodness ultimately in God, from which flows our understanding of the kind of goodness that God desires for humanity and the kind of goodness we are to pursue for others and ourselves. As Micah

---

23. Rensberger, "Love of God as the Source of Spirituality and Justice," 45.

reminds us, what God deems good and desirous is justice, lovingkindness, and wise humility. These are good not just because God requires them but because their bearings on the lives of others are good. Others need us to do justice, to be faithful and humbly wise, in order for there to be growing conditions of goodness.

God desires that humans flourish in our creaturely existence as God intended, able to live lives that are fruitful, integrated, meaningful, and productive in service to God and others. In order for this to happen, humans require certain goods necessary for flourishing, such things as adequate resources to meet the necessities of life—food, shelter, work, and life-giving relationships, to name a few. The work of justice involves attending to these basic needs of human life. In order for us to participate in embodying God's goodness and helping others enjoy the goodness that God desires, we need to develop moral sensitivities and capacities that take on the concerns of others. Moral formation is a process by which we grow in these capacities to see, hear, and respond to the concerns of others based on our commitments to do what God requires, to love what God loves, and to do what God does.

In moral psychology, a bit of a skirmish developed between the thought of Lawrence Kohlberg and Carol Gilligan over the ways in which persons are morally formed and exercise moral reasoning. Kohlberg's stages of moral reasoning end with justice as the normative and most mature stage of moral development.[24] This sixth and final stage of moral reasoning is attained when an individual can make judgments that are universal, impartial, and equitable. A position of objectivity is necessary in order for moral judgments about what is just, fair, and equitable to occur. So while one must be able to put one's self in the shoes of another, it is the principle of justice that guides moral reasoning, not his or her relationship to the other. Gilligan's critique of Kohlberg is primarily twofold:[25] one, Kohlberg's subjects were boys, and two, inattention to the ways in which girls are socialized into different modes of moral reasoning neglects a fundamental aspect of relationships, namely, care. Gilligan offers an "ideal of care" as "an activity of relationship, of seeing and responding to need, taking care of the world by sustaining the web of connection so that no one is left alone."[26] Both Kohlberg and Gilligan offer fruitful insights pertinent for

24. See Kohlberg, *Philosophy of Moral Development*.

25. See Gilligan, *In a Different Voice*.

26. Ibid., 62.

appreciating dynamics of the moral life. Kohlberg's placement of justice as a high standard of moral reflection and judgment is important, and Gilligan's emphasis on care as a moral criterion is necessary given human relationality. However, Kohlberg's somewhat abstract conception of justice is devoid of its relational contexts and the requirement to *do* justice, whereas Gilligan may inadvertently present a gendered notion of care, and hence morality, that consigns care to women *because* we are women.

Is there a way to bring justice and care together that is more reflective of the kind of justice that God desires, which has as its aim the good of others? For Leonardo Boff, it is possible if we reframe these criteria as "care with justice."[27] This combination of justice and care is based on an understanding of humanity that is both relational and oriented toward goods such as justice and love. Boff writes:

> The human being is fundamentally an entity of affection, bearer of *pathos*, of the capacity to feel, to affect and to be affected. It possesses intellectual reasoning, *logos*, but it is also gifted with emotional reasoning, with sensibility reasoning and spiritual reasoning. The human being is a being-with-the-others and for-the-others in the world. The human being does not exist in isolation in its magnificent autonomy; it rather lives within a web of concrete relations and always finds itself connected to this web. The human being does not require a social contract to live with others; rather, the human being already lives in community.[28]

This combination of care with justice honors the concrete and relational dimensions of our existence yet allows justice to guide the quality and shape of how we form and live in these relationships. This is not a male or female way of morally reasoning. It is a human way, a good way, which acknowledges the diverse dimensions of our contexts, the variety of human needs, and the concrete commitments within our web of relationships that require doing justice, loving kindness, and walking with humble wisdom.

Another important insight offered by social science theorists such as Kohlberg and Gilligan is that we are socialized into moral values and ways of reasoning. Even though we might affirm a care with justice, we need to be socialized—discipled, if you will—into learning how to care and take on the concerns of others that attend to justice. This assumes a place and a network of relationships that hold care with justice in high regard as a

27. Boff, *Virtues for Another Possible World*, 259. Italics in original.

28. Ibid., 258–59.

moral norm in Christian faith—and the willingness to pay attention to this norm in ethical reflection, deliberation, and practice, as well as the willingness to risk putting this norm into practice. Our dispositions and habits can be formed as we are socialized into particular ways of seeing and living in the world by learning to hear, see, and take on the concerns of others so that we might justly care for them. Developing a capacity to care is crucial for moral maturity and involves the ongoing formation of compassion and empathy. Spohn defines compassion and empathy in the following way: "*Empathy* refers to the affective, imaginative and cognitive capacity that enables us to enter and identify with the experience of others. *Compassion* refers to the most active and engaged form of empathy, namely, that disposition directed particularly to those in great need or suffering."[29]

This capacity for and need for empathy and compassion is also noted by social psychologists and is particularly pertinent for our global contexts, where interdependencies are more evident in the breaking and blurring of boundaries that comes with globalization.[30] Compassion and empathy are not virtues we can assume to exist, especially given that one of the sad ironies of globalization is the reifying and further solidification of national, ethnic, and religious boundaries seeking to separate "us" from "them." Compassion and empathy must be and can be learned by minimizing distance that can take many forms. Attending to our language that caricatures a "them" and a "they" is an important first step. Willingness to hear the stories and experiences of those who suffer due to the actions of others is important for expanding our abilities to hear and see. Imagining ourselves in situations not of our own choosing, where our deepest vulnerabilities and needs are exposed, is part of learning compassion and empathy. Placing ourselves in the space of others as friends in solidarity helps foster compassion and empathy.[31]

By the grace of God, the example of Jesus, and the power of the Holy Spirit, our "moral myopia" that narrows our interests and concerns can be corrected as we learn new perceptions and experience "a transformation of basic moral dispositions as a precondition to widening one's perspective."[32] As Spohn asks, "What would it take to expand a self-absorbed person to

29. Spohn, *Go and Do Likewise*, 90. Italics in original.

30. See the interesting collection of essays in Scuzzarello, Kinnvall, and Renwick-Monroe, *On Behalf of Others*.

31. See Pohl and Heuertz, *Friendship at the Margins*.

32. Spohn, *Go and Do Likewise*, 106–7.

become alert to the independent realities of others? How could a defensive person become tolerant of those who have different values?"[33] These are crucial questions that get at the heart of forming our capacities and dispositions for compassion and empathy, which will eventually require practices that are morally forming.

Forming Dispositions and Capacities to Act

The second implication from this theological reflection on Micah 6:6–8 concerns the relationships between what we desire and how we act. Micah orients us to the right things to desire based on God's requirement and call to do justice, love kindness, and walk in humility with God. The relationship between desires, affections, dispositions, and actions is foundational to virtue ethics with its focus on who we are, who we are becoming, how we become good, and how we act. According to Aristotle, one of its classic articulators, the essence of virtue ethics is the acquisition of virtues, or those qualities that make a person good and that enable one to achieve a life of happiness, or excellence, as the ultimate goal of one's life. Virtues are internal character qualities as well as external in that they are learned and manifested, furthering one's growth in virtue through habits and practices. As Aristotle's theory of virtue is essentially social, so is virtue from a Christian perspective.[34] The formation of virtue occurs in a web of multiple relationships: in relationship with the Triune God, against the backdrop of a Christian narrative, in a community that attempts to appropriate the Scriptures on an ongoing and faithful basis, and in practices that help form us in virtuous ways. As Christian spirituality is public and social, so is Christian morality. Virtues cannot be constrained to a sense of personal morality that focuses on the attainment of pious personal characteristics. It makes no sense for us to describe ourselves as loving, kind, gentle, and compassionate when there is no significant community in which we are learning these virtues and putting them into practice, and when there is no community able to discern if we are *actually* becoming more loving, kind, gentle, and compassionate.

The constructed divide between "an ethic of being" and an "ethic of doing" is foreign to the Scriptures and an anomaly in Christian moral

33. Ibid., 107.

34. See my interaction with and critique of Aristotle's theory of virtue in the context of Christian ethics in chapter 4 of my *Reviving Evangelical Ethics*.

thought. As Micah reminds us, justice is not a virtuous quality we are to think about; it is something we are to do. Loving mercy is not a one-sided acceptance of God's mercy toward us; it is a virtue we are to desire and practice in extending mercy to others. Walking humbly with God is what we do as we practice faith, hope, and love in relationships with God and with others, recognizing our dependence on God as a good thing and our interdependence and relational commitments with others (and theirs with us) as morally significant. James, in one of the earliest letters to Christian communities, draws on the intricate relationship between our identity as God's people and how we are to act as God's people when he writes, "But be doers of the word, and not merely hearers who deceive themselves" (Jas 1:22), since "faith by itself, if it has no works, is dead" (2:17). To allay the fear that some Protestants may have that virtue may be a form of "works righteousness," it is important to locate virtues in God's grace and the impartation of God's power to live our lives as God desires (1 Pet 1:3–11).[35] While virtues may not be a means by which we earn God's favor, they are certainly what God desires and what God makes possible through the Holy Spirit as we follow Christ. As spirituality has crucial public dimensions in that it is visible and observable, so, too, do Christian virtues necessitate social expressions. Christian morality cannot be encapsulated in abstract moral principles *about* justice, mercy, and personal piety. Christian morality is learned and lived out through the formation of right desire *and* right actions that are consonant with our deepest beliefs and affections. It is an embodied way of life that is learned, lived, and expressed in complex social spaces.

Corporate Dimensions: Becoming Wise Moral Actors

All of us live as actors (and as those acted upon) in social contexts. We are constrained and shaped by the contexts and communities in which our identities are formed, our relationships are established (or broken), and our moral sensibilities are learned. We also have influence, to various degrees, in determining the qualities and goods of our communities. Most of us are members of diverse communities at church, in neighborhoods, in places of employment, and in institutions we serve. It is inevitable, and necessary, that our lives bump up against others. The fact that we share space and resources with others makes social spaces moral ones, necessitating our

35. See the helpful work by Kotva, *Christian Case for Virtue Ethics*.

abilities and competencies to navigate complex moral spaces with wisdom and integrity.

The learning and practicing of wisdom, the third implication for this scriptural reflection on moral formation, is an important virtue in Christian ethics that enables us to put into practice what we affirm as just and necessary for human flourishing. Wisdom is the capacity to discern how to act, and when, in ways appropriate to the needs we are addressing and the contexts in which these needs occur. Wisdom is not simply a cognitive enterprise; it involves knowing what to do in the particularities, complexities, and contingencies of any given situation.[36] Wisdom is a virtue to be desired and diligently sought after, one necessary for understanding how we are to live in ways that please God in our shared desires for righteousness and justice (Proverbs 2). As LeRon Shults notes, "Wise persons are identified not simply by the propositional content of their intellects but by the way in which they bind themselves in fiduciary relations within community. . . . We become wise as we come into a transforming relation with divine wisdom, in which we are invited to share in the intimacy of the dynamic knowledge and being known that is the life of the infinitely faithful trinitarian God."[37] Micah reminds us that wisdom starts with the humble recognition of our need for God and the importance of nurturing our relationships with God in order to know more fully what God desires. Wisdom does require knowing what God desires and how God wants us to live. Even as we affirm the goal of our lives as the ongoing transformation of our desires and affections, this transformation cannot occur without knowledge of these desires, their source, content, and importance, as well as the committed and practiced means by which we act according to what we know is right, good, noble, true, and just.

This makes the acquisition of wisdom intensely practical, captured in the notion of *phronesis*, or practical wisdom. Van der Ven, borrowing from Paul Ricoeur, proposes the recognition of two necessary dimensions of practical wisdom: singularity and contingency.[38] Singularity is necessary for us to apply moral norms in particular situations. Not all situations are the same. Wisdom enables us to perceive the unique dynamics at play, the particular needs to be addressed, the root causes of issues, and what is appropriate and fitting for *this* particular situation. For example, while we

36. See van der Ven, *Formation of the Moral Self*, 76–79.
37. Shults and Sandage, *Transforming Spirituality*, 71.
38. Van der Ven, *Formation of the Moral Self*, 77.

might espouse love of neighbor as a moral norm, practical wisdom presses us to discern who my neighbor is, what is the cause of my neighbor's distress, what does my neighbor need, and what is just and right for my neighbor in *this particular situation*. Practical wisdom helps us navigate the contingences of any given situation, its open-endedness and unpredictability. Espousing moral absolutes is an easy task. Putting into practice our moral claims in complex, contingent, and corporate contexts filled with a variety of personalities, problems, possibilities, and pitfalls is quite another. The ability to do justice and love mercy requires wisdom that comes from God, received with humility and trust in order to live out our moral claims.

As a virtue, wisdom is learned and practiced. Early on in my vocation as a Christian ethicist, I posed the following question to a trusted and dear friend who is also a Christian ethicist: "What does it mean to be a person who not just teaches students in a seminary Christian ethics but one who is a Christian ethicist and a member in this particular institution?" I was struggling with discerning my responsibilities to my colleagues and institution given the vocational commitments I had made as a Christian ethicist. Her response was wise and helpful. She suggested we start by a willingness to ask questions that others might not want to ask or are afraid to ask. Often, posing basic questions about how power works, how decisions are made, who benefits from particular institutional arrangements and decisions, and who is harmed by them is an important first step for raising the spectrum of our moral awareness of practices we tend to take for granted. Yet my dear colleague and friend would also caution that this necessitates practical wisdom in knowing how to address issues, to whom, why and when, especially when confronting issues of the abuse of power and injustice in our communities. Knowing what to do is important. Knowing how to put into practice what we believe requires the wisdom acquired and learned from God as we seek to align our lives with what God desires.

Conclusion

It is difficult to keep these three concepts of Christian morality separate since they are so necessarily related. Christian moral formation is guided by a desire for the right things: the desire for what God desires in doing justice, loving mercy, and walking humbly as we seek wisdom and understanding. These desires give shape to the Christian moral life in the growing capacity to justly care about the good of others, an attention to both who we are and what we do. We need practical wisdom to aid us in acting rightly in complex and contested moral spaces as we strive to do justice, love mercy, and walk humbly with God. I hope the parallels between spirituality and morality are becoming more obvious as we learn to desire God and to grasp the things that God desires. Turning to a discussion on practices will, I hope, make these connections even clearer.

three

Practices: Integration of Spirituality and Morality

IN COLLEGE, I WAS involved in a weekly Bible study with friends as we studied the book of Ephesians. What I remember about this experience was the predominant emphasis on "our position in Christ" based on Ephesians 1 and the preponderant use of the expression "in Christ." Perhaps this focus was important given an audience of college students bombarded with images of selves valued by market advertising and at the point of making significant career choices upon graduation. I recall that a strong subtext of this focused study was the assumption that there is nothing we can do to please God but to rest in our position of being "in Christ." My roommate attended this study with me a couple of times. She was disturbed by the assumptions that seemed to undergird this focus for its potential to foster an acceptance of the blessings bestowed on us "in Christ" without the accompanying commitments to do the "good works, which God prepared beforehand to be our way of life" (Eph 2:10).

She was right to be concerned. As the years have passed since my college days, I, too, have become concerned with some of the fragmentations between how we understand the relationships between what God has done for us in Christ, our Christian identities, the formation of our character, the kinds of concerns that we should take on because we are "in Christ," and the kind of lives we are called to lead. My roommate's concern reflected the critique that Wolterstorff offers referenced in the last chapter: "The biblical critique of humankind is that we live with the illusion that we can get the blessing without the ethic and that the blessing will be enough for the flourishing—believing, in turn, that the way to secure the blessing without the ethic is to engage in the actions of the cult."[1]

In the first two chapters, I explored Christian spirituality and morality to establish an integrative framework for these two important aspects of Christian faith and practice. Even though I attended to each separately, I hope that their interrelatedness was evident. It was difficult to keep the boundaries between the two intact. It was not easy to talk about one without talking about the other since there is such an important bond between the sources for Christian spirituality and morality, and the directions to which they point us. Both are grounded in God as the source of goodness and God's desires; both are patterned after the life of Christ; both are empowered by the Holy Spirit; and both encompass all aspects of life. The blurring between spiritual and moral formation is important to maintain lest we see either process as tidy, compact, and contained. In this chapter, I will make the connections between spirituality and morality more evident. I will also start a discussion on practices as important intersections that bring spirituality and morality together in a tighter and more interdependent relationship.

The Integration and Interplay of Spirituality and Morality

The relationship between spirituality and morality is succinctly described by Gula as this: "Spirituality without morality is disembodied; morality without spirituality is rootless."[2] Spirituality requires embodiment, and morality requires grounding in sources such as Scripture, theology, and community, which give shape to our ultimate desires to be in relationship with the living God and to participate in God's good work in the world. Morality needs a norming source of transcendence offered by Christian spirituality. Spirituality needs a content and context to give form to its practice and purpose.

By way of recap, spiritual and moral shaping involve the formation of desire. Our desire is for God and the things of God. What God desires ought to be the right things that we desire. Spirituality and morality need a *telos*, a robust vision of the purposes to which our lives are oriented and which guide us in ways of living as these purposes become a part of who we are and incarnated in what we do. Scripture provides this for morality and

1. Wolterstorff, "Justice as a Condition of Authentic Liturgy," in *Hearing the Call*, 51.
2. Gula, *Call to Holiness*, 5.

spirituality, resulting in an interrelationship between the two. Both have an outward focus. Neither spirituality nor morality is constrained to private spaces of our lives that focus *just* on our relationships with God or *inward* growth in piety. While these aspects are important, authentic spirituality and morality draw us outward, so that we freely and justly take on concern for others. Spiritual and moral formation involves the mutual shaping of our affections, dispositions, and behavior. Spirituality does not privilege being over doing, nor does morality focus on doing over being. Who we are (and who we are becoming) is related to what we do, the choices we make, the experiences we are willing to enter, and the risks we take. What we do shapes who we are. Spirituality and morality both have embodied, important corporate dimensions that are lived out before others in responsible, life-giving, and justice-honoring relationships. Both are concerned with ways of living, with growth in wisdom, and with fostering loyalty so that we might live according to what God requires and to our deepest desires. As Bill Cosgrove aptly summarizes,

> The basic point to keep in mind is that the spiritual and the moral are not to be found in two separate compartments of our Christian lives as we live them. In fact, they are so closely related and intertwined that they cannot be adequately distinguished in a way that would allow one to list their characteristics or elements in two quite distinct categories. Rather in profound ways the spiritual is moral and the moral is spiritual or, at the very least, our spiritual experiences underpin and provide energy for our moral values, virtues and commitments. At the same time, our moral experiences express, ratify, deepen and even correct our vision of life with its basic attitudes and values, in and through which we live out our love and commitment to God and our neighbor.[3]

Bringing spirituality and morality together in our conceptual categories is one thing. Bringing them together in actual practice and mutually forming experiences can be quite another. I turn now to explore the concept of practices for the ways in which they provide an intersection for understanding the relationships between spiritual disciplines and ethical practices.

3. Cosgrove, "Relating Spirituality and Morality," 31.

Practices: Intersections for Spirituality and Morality

Practices are a means by which we bring together what we believe and what we desire with what we do. Practices are just as much about forming us morally and spiritually as they are about extending and embodying our beliefs in ways that reflect God's concerns and commitment to the world.[4] In his work on virtue ethics, Alasdair MacIntyre emphasizes the importance of practices for living out the narratives of our lives. Practices are essential parts of traditions that function to train and form us as well as express the stories by which we live. MacIntyre writes, "By a 'practice' I am going to mean any coherent and complex form of socially established cooperative human activity through which goods internal to that form of activity are realized in the course of trying to achieve those standards of excellence which are appropriate to, and partially definitive of, that form of activity, with the result that human powers to achieve excellence, and human conceptions of the ends and goods involved, are systematically extended."[5]

Allow me to break down MacIntyre's definition of a practice in order to move toward explicit application to how practices bring together spirituality and morality. First, practices lend coherence by providing a link between means, or what we do, and our desires and the ends that orients our lives. The relationship between means and ends is important in moral thought, lest we default to heavily pragmatic ethical considerations that focus on results without regard to how we achieve these results. It is the means that tend to be morally and spiritually forming. *How* and *why* we do what we do is just as important as *what* we want to achieve. Second, practices carry with them the vision, "the standards of excellence," toward which they point, which is why practices themselves should be well thought through. Practices ought to be guided by the excellencies of our moral vision as we understand it based on God's desires and intentions, not by pragmatism or convenience.

Third, practices are not random things we do but are guided and informed by what we understand the desired end to be, thereby lending an observable consonance between means and ends. Practices carry the message of what we believe. They offer a public picture of our ultimate desires and how we live out these desires in the things we *actually* do. In doing

---

4. Parts of this section are from a plenary paper I was asked to present in March 2010 at the meeting of the Midwest Region of the Evangelical Theological Society held at Bethel Seminary in St. Paul, Minnesota, on "What Makes Praxis Evangelical?"

5. MacIntyre, *After Virtue*, 187.

so, practices both embody *and* extend the "ends and goods" of the story by which we live. For Christians, this story is narrated in Scripture. It is the story of God's reconciling love offered in Christ, the "visible expression of the invisible God" (Col 1:15–23), who inaugurated the reign of God, inviting us in through repentance and faith to receive this good news of salvation and participate in the redeeming work that God is doing in the restoration of creation. This *euangelion* is heralded in word and embodied in communities of faith who by confession have submitted themselves to the lordship of Christ. The people of God are now the "signpost" of the kingdom of God,[6] a "peculiar people,"[7] who proclaim *and* "perform" the kingdom of God[8] and who embody the "politics of Jesus."[9] Our moral framework as those who have experienced the redeeming grace of God in Christ and who have been invited to participate in what God wants to do in the world is grounded in God's own Trinitarian life, guided by the vision of the kingdom of God, with our ethical practices informed by the ways of Jesus and empowered by the Holy Spirit.[10]

Finally, practices are social and cooperative human activities that train persons in how to live out what they believe and, in doing so, make a profound impact on the lives of other persons, including those performing the practice. We may conceive of these practices as spiritual disciplines and activities necessary for Christian discipleship, things we do that help us establish new habits and ways of living more responsively to God and others. Disciplines such as prayer, study, meditation, service, and worship train us. We do spiritual disciplines in our bodies: we may kneel for prayer; we may sit for long periods of time for study; we remain quiet when we meditate; we get out of our chairs for service; and we gather with other bodies for corporate worship. Because spiritual disciplines are embodied, they foster a deeper sense of our moral obligations to God and others by placing us in closer proximity to others. We cannot claim the aim of spiritual formation to be growth in Christ-likeness, friendship with God, and maturation in the Spirit, without the accompanying commitments to take on the concerns of God as evidence that we are growing in our friendships with God. Spiritual formation ought to heighten our moral sensibilities and passions, while

6. Snyder, *Community of the King.*

7. Clapp, *Peculiar People.*

8. Chilton and McDonald, *Jesus and the Ethics of the Kingdom.*

9. Yoder, *Politics of Jesus.*

10. See the important work by Stassen and Gushee, *Kingdom Ethics.*

moral formation reinforces our need for wisdom, strength, and courage to put into practice what we believe.

Dorothy Bass and Craig Dykstra offer a more explicit and accessible definition of Christian practices. For Bass and Dykstra, practices are "things Christian people do together over time to address fundamental human needs in response to and in light of God's active presence for the life of the world."[11] Bass and Dykstra offer this definition to give us "a way of thinking about how a way of life that is deeply responsive to God's grace takes *actual* shape among human beings."[12] Practices are grounded in our response to God's presence and work, often identified as important motivation for spiritual formation. Practices are also the way in which we respond to human need in light of what we understand God to be about in the world, which gives impetus to our ethical concerns and moral action. As Gula writes, "Spiritual practices should bring us to a heightened sensitivity to our moral responsibilities, and moral living should return us to our spiritual practices where we focus ourselves on our ultimate dependence on God. To deal with spiritual and moral practices in this reciprocal way affirms the inseparability of the love of God and love of neighbor."[13] Yet Gula also offers an appropriate caution lest we oversimplify the processes of spiritual and moral formation and thin out the relationship between the two:

> The connections between spiritual practices and the moral life are complex, not simple. While spiritual practices can keep alive our relationship with God, it takes practical moral decisions and the habit of moral practices to implement our spiritual relationship and vision. Moreover, since our personal and cultural experiences are also at stake in determining moral character and choice, spiritual practices do not have a monopoly on our morality. Given the many factors that influence our moral development and given the fact that not everyone engages common practices with the same depth of commitment to their meaning, we cannot expect practices to ensure a certain kind of moral character and behavior.[14]

I agree with Gula, and I am not suggesting that practices "ensure a certain kind of moral character and behavior." As a Christian ethicist, I appreciate Gula's caution lest we reduce either spirituality or morality to

11. Dykstra and Bass, "Theological Understanding of Christian Practices," 18.

12. Ibid., 15. Italics mine.

13. Gula, *Call to Holiness*, 148.

14. Ibid., 156.

simple solutions to complex issues. I mentioned in the introduction that we cannot draw a seamless line between a theological or moral claim and a practice, nor can we make simple jumps by reducing problems to just spiritual ones. Thankfully, Christian morality and spirituality are far richer and more demanding than this.

In his *Outline of a Theory of Practice*, Pierre Bourdieu cautions that anyone who purports to make objective claims about practices in any given context does so as a privileged outsider, unaware of or indifferent to the multiple interpretations of symbols, the complexity of human motives, and "foreign" standards of logic based on ethnocentricity.[15] We ought not to see a practice as a "mechanical reaction" or as random and freewheeling.[16] Bourdieu instead suggests that we see an important dialectical relationship between *habitus* and practices. *Habitus* is a collection of dispositions, ideas, and values shared by a group that create an "objective structure"—what we might call "culture"—that more often than not works below our consciousness as we accept "objective structures" as normative.[17] This *habitus* then produces a variety of collective practices. For Bourdieu, both *habitus* and practices are complex and multilayered; neither can be reduced for the sake of simplicity, ease, and convenience. Nor can they be simplified by an act of power by those who rely on prescribed practices to legitimate official statements and structures, insisting that practices are meant to be strict and normative.[18] A simplistic understanding of the relationships between *habitus* and practices often results in an unhealthy conformity and uncritical acceptance of "what is" as "what should be" since both *habitus* and practices are not subject to ongoing ethical analysis. Questioning and dissent, for the purposes of discovering richer and perhaps more faithful practices, are quelled for the purposes of fostering compliance and maintaining a veneer of unified acceptance of official statements and sanctioned practices.

I heed the cautions from Gula and Bourdieu. My aim is not to come up with normative practices that are simple and seamless and then superimposed on any context at any time. My hope is to present practices as an important way of reconnecting and reintegrating the relationships between spirituality and moral life that have too often been compartmentalized and viewed as distinct processes of Christian formation. When morality and

15. Bourdieu, *Outline of a Theory of Practice*.

16. Ibid., 73.

17. Ibid., 78–83.

18. Ibid., 39–40.

spirituality are compartmentalized and simplified, Gula's and Bourdieu's fears are confirmed. Spirituality and morality are oversimplified and flattened for convenience, and we cease to engage in the critical reflection so necessary for Christian formation.

I see practices as a means by which we concretize our spiritual and ethical commitments. Or, as Jamie Smith notes, practices that become habits "constitute the *fulcrum* of our desire: they are the hinge that 'turns' our heart, our love, such that it is predisposed to be aimed in certain directions."[19] Spiritually and morally formative practices reflect and reform our desires, commitments, and dispositions. As Spohn writes: "Both moral and spiritual practices set us up for the right dispositions. They channel good intentions into habitual behavior, and those habits evoke and train the dispositions of the heart. . . . Habits that are reflectively entered into shape character. Over time regular practices can strengthen commitments so we enact them with a certain ease and even delight. Attentively performed habits lead to the formation of moral dispositions."[20]

Spiritual disciplines and ethical practices require a willingness to reflect on our current conditions with openness and honesty before God in order to see reality for what it is. They necessitate a willingness to see, perceive, and respond to the needs around us. They entail courage and trust to step out in faith and experimentation in our attempt to respond to human need. Practices call for wisdom and discernment in order to understand what to do in *this* particular context in *this* particular time. Spiritual and moral formation require time to think together, to pray, to discern, and to find wisdom for knowing how to bring our moral claims together in contested and complex moral spaces. They need a Christian community, a place where we learn to embody the compassion and empathy that must come with interdependence. Both spiritual and moral formation are "other" centered—centered on God and on others in our communities whose needs often cry out to us as they do to God. Bringing together spiritual and moral formation in a dynamic relation is crucial to integrity, the ongoing integrating into wholeness of ourselves and our communities as we live by faith and hopeful anticipation, and as we embody love for God and neighbor as the greatest of all desires (1 Cor 13).

This interrelationship between spirituality and morality fostered by practices that are mutually forming is an important aspect of maturity and

19. Smith, *Desiring the Kingdom*, 56.
20. Spohn, *Go and Do Likewise*, 39.

well-being. A mature spirituality incorporates a robust morality. A commitment to justice is one of the six marks of a healthy spirituality suggested by William Callahan. Note the moral dimensions of these signs of a healthy, mature spirituality. It is built on actual experience that enables us to follow Christ. It is simple, deep, loving, strong, and durable. Mature spirituality is socially conscious and hospitable in our embrace of a world that God still loves and works to redeem.[21] On the relationship between spiritual maturity and ethical consciousness, Callahan writes that we cannot "rest any longer with a purely personal vision of faith, whether its focus be 'me and Jesus' or an attempt to restrict our concerns to interpersonal relationships. Interpersonal relationships are good, but they are simply incomplete, just as adolescents with their preoccupation with themselves have not yet matured. . . . [T]he most powerful, and still emerging, modern development in faith and spirituality is the call to develop a societal consciousness and commitment to support the work of justice, which is now seen, not as on the periphery of faith, but at the core of a healthy, adult faith."[22]

This relationship between spirituality, morality, and maturity is also explored by Shults and Sandage in their coauthored book, *Transforming Spirituality: Integrating Theology and Psychology*. According to Sandage, a "health-conducive" spirituality has a number of dimensions. He identifies five:

1. intentionally embodied
2. developmentally generative
3. relationally connected
4. justice enhancing
5. narratively coherent[23]

His insights are important for the ways we conceive of practices as crucial for bringing spiritual and moral formation together in a dynamic, healthy relationship. Practices are embodied in the things we actually do that reflect what we profess to believe. They aid in creating a narrative coherence to our lives, which we so desperately need for wholeness and integrity. Practices are generative in that they hold before us challenges for exploration, growth, experimentation, and trust, enabling us to grow and develop in our

21. Callahan, "Spirituality and Justice," 150–54.

22. Ibid., 153–54.

23. Shults and Sandage, *Transforming Spirituality*, 210.

relationships with God and with others. Practices draw us to our relational connections, especially if we see them as our response to God and to human need. Practices are "justice enhancing," an important contribution from Sandage, a psychologist, to our conceptions of how an integrative spiritual maturity and mental health result in active concern for others. He writes, "In a world teeming with poverty, malnutrition, ethnic hatred, disease, and oppression, spirituality will be health-conducive at the systemic level only if it is justice-enhancing. That is, healthy spirituality should move people toward compassionate alterity or a widening circle of concern for others."[24]

A healthy spirituality, according to Sandage, or a holistic spirituality, according to Brad Kallenberg, has a strong, inherent moral component. For Kallenberg, individualistic spirituality is a "misnomer" since a healthy, authentic spirituality requires a community in which individuals are shaped and trained in the practices of the church. Christian spirituality is, therefore, inherently social.[25] Kallenberg writes that "*social practices are the form that spirituality takes,* and *social practices are the form that social justice takes.*"[26] This reaffirms my claim that Christian spirituality and morality take particular shapes in the form of practices that are visible in justice-enhancing ways. Appropriate to Gula's and Bordieu's concerns, practices are complex, socially constituted, and narrative dependent. They are not automatic, mechanical, or random. Practices require that we think and discern together in imaginative ways about who we are and how we should live. In doing so, we are formed spiritually and morally as our awareness of God and God's concerns for the world are heightened.

Practices as Forming, Extending, and Resisting

I see practices as critical for forming our spirituality, moral sensibilities, and ethical practices. In this regard, practices work in three particular ways. First, practices form, train, and orient us by helping us establish habits that are conducive to spiritual and moral growth.[27] As such, practices are akin to what are classically referred to as spiritual disciplines, which are means by which we cooperate with God in our spiritual and moral growth. This

24. Ibid., 212.

25. Kallenberg, "Holistic Spirituality as Witness," 78.

26. Ibid., 82. Italics in original.

27. Spohn notes that spiritual practices are pedagogical and transformational for the formation of a reflective, authentic spirituality. See *Go and Do Likewise*, 36–42.

divine-human cooperation is important to maintain for appreciating practices as *human* responses to God's active presence in the world. Practices help us break patterns and establish new ones. Practices require that we think about what we do in light of what we believe. Practices, like spiritual disciplines, require self-examination, an acknowledgment of shortcomings and failures, and an openness to the new work that God desires for all creation. While it may be tempting to value the end result of a practice for the good it might bring to others, it is just as important to see the good inherent in the practice for the ways in which those who are participating in the practice are changed. In MacIntyre's definition of a practice, there is value and good inherent in the *doing* of the practice that offers its own rewards and benefits regardless of the outcome. Bass and Dykstra remind us that while practices have practical purposes in meeting human needs, their value does not rest solely in their results. About our own participation in practices, they write:

> Just taking a full and earnest part in them is somehow good in itself, even when purposes that are visible to the human eye are not achieved. If one patient dies unrelieved in spirit as well as body, do healers abandon the practice when the next patient needs help? No, they do not, for they understand what they do as part of the practice of God. They are doing it not just because it works (though they hope it does) but because it is good. The observable outcome is, in a sense, beyond them; a different satisfaction comes just from taking part.[28]

This is important to remember for grasping how practices form, train, and orient us, particularly in contexts that are highly programmatic in understanding how humans actually change. Practices take time, attention, deliberation, conversation, experimentation, and risk. These are goods that practices carry regardless of the outcome. Taking time, paying attention, deliberating with others, and taking risks are practices in themselves that may heighten our spiritual and moral sensibilities.

Practices bring together cognitive and experiential dimensions of spiritual and moral formation. We think about what we believe and how to respond, while at the same time experimenting and risking in our practices for the shaping of experience even as we still work out beliefs and understandings. I'm always struck by the risks that Jesus took with the disciples in this regard. We know that even at the end of the Synoptic Gospels and

28. Dykstra and Bass, "Times of Yearning, Practices of Faith," 7.

into Acts the disciples were still unclear and confused about Jesus' identity and mission. They had not correctly "filled in the blanks" in the book of discipleship. The resurrection was an illusion and false hope until Jesus appeared to them. Yet, during the disciples' time and training with Jesus, they were still asked to go and practice what Jesus valued: healing, preaching, compassion, and feeding the hungry. In spite of what the disciples actually knew and believed, they performed concrete actions and, in doing so, fostered degrees of goods and help for those they served. They practiced what Jesus preached and, one hopes, grew in their understanding of Jesus' identity and mission.

Practices, therefore, can create a paradigm for spiritual and moral formation by bringing together the cognitive and experiential, weaving them together in mutually forming ways that work to orient and train us in the ways of Christ. This creates possibilities for contexts where formation is a highly cognitive endeavor, assuming that somehow "right information" will result in "right behavior." While on the pastoral staff of a church, I was the Director of Outreach working with the Director of Small Groups. We became concerned about the navel-gazing occurring in small groups, which was based on the assumption that Christian formation was about getting right information and being able to relate to people with similar issues and concerns. We implemented a proposal and strategy that requested that current small groups and ones in the process of being formed adopt a service commitment as part of their identity and common purpose. Service is a means to Christian formation and builds community among those serving together even as awareness of the needs in our communities grows and impels our conceptions of Christian spirituality and morality outward. Christian community does not (only) exist to meet the needs of its members but to extend Christ's love and compassion to others. Practices offer possibilities in contexts where experience is unchallenged and unexamined by actual beliefs. Christian formation requires belief and doing, and practices provide a more dynamic way of conceiving of the relationship between spirituality and morality given an emphasis on the things we do in response to God.

Second, practices extend our beliefs and make them visible to others. For MacIntyre, practices extend narratives and traditions, enabling them to live on and "tell" the story of our traditions. For Dykstra and Bass, practices have histories and traditions rooted in practices of Christian communities in our attempts to live faithfully before God, according to Scripture, and in healthy community with others. They write:

Enter a Christian practice, and you will find that you are part of a community that has been doing this thing for centuries—not doing it as well as it should, to be sure, but doing it steadily, in conscious continuity with stories of the Bible and in frequent conversation about how to do it better. You join by jumping in where you are: learning the hymns, volunteering to welcome the homeless, seeking companions who will support you in prayer as you say yes to God and no to destructive forces in your life. Once in, you find that a practice has a certain internal feel and momentum. It is ancient, and larger than you are; it weaves you together with other people in doing things none of us could do alone. But each practice is also ever new, taking fresh form each day as it subtly adapts to find expression in every neighborhood and land.[29]

For Protestants, two practices that are routine parts of congregations are the Lord's Supper and Baptism.[30] We participate in these practices regularly because of how central they are to our faith and our belief in the life, death, and resurrection of Christ. These practices "preach" this primary story of our lives in word and deed, and in doing so, they extend our traditions, making them visible to those who are participants and witnesses. Practices also help us reflect on all sorts of things we do together that embody and belie what we believe. Allow me to offer an example. I was on the pastoral staff of a church in the early 1990s. This was a new church plant that was using a school auditorium for worship services. We had a desire to host large congregational gatherings over a meal but did not have space at our disposal. We rented space in a local hotel for a meal, which required using their food services. This resulted in a cost of thirty dollars per person for dinner (or fifty dollars for couples, a practice I still find highly annoying and problematic!). This decision was made by persons who would not have difficulty paying thirty dollars for a meal, without regard for members of the congregation for whom this would be a hardship. What became clear in our deliberations was this: persons were not meant to be excluded by a prohibitive cost, but we simply did not think about the actual practice and its unintended outcome of exclusion. In our practice, we were committing a 1 Corinthians 11 sin (and likely other ones!), in that those without financial means were unable to participate in the fellowship meal. By allowing

---

29. Ibid.

30. See the rich collection of essays in Hauerwas and Wells, *Blackwell Companion to Christian Ethics*, for the relationships between worship, liturgical practices, the sacraments, and Christian ethics.

Scripture to challenge an assumed practice of simply renting hotel space for a fellowship meal, we reversed course and asked persons to pay what they were able so that all could participate. We had more than enough to pay the expenses for the meal. My point in raising this example is this: practices flowing from our serious, open, and communal engagement with Scripture can always be dynamic, challenged, and changed. Practices drive us back to our primary engagement with Scripture, the traditions of the church, human needs, and our contemporary contexts, prodding us to more faithful ways of embodying our traditions for our times as we respond to the needs of others.

Third, practices enable us to resist dominant trends and ideologies that co-opt our faith and derail our faithful living in the world. Not only do they help us foster habits in order to incarnate our commitments and God's concerns, but they also enable us to work against the grain of what would be acceptable, easy, and expedient. Practices offer alternative ways of living that push back on harmful practices that affect other human beings. This has been an important insight offered by theologians and ethicists on practices of Sabbath keeping.[31] Sabbath keeping is not simply a day of rest for burned-out and weary workers. It is a day of resistance to the all-pervasive ideologies of consumerism, frenetic work, unbridled use of the earth's resources, and the desire to accumulate more, whatever (and to whomever) the cost. L. Roger Owens suggests that Sabbath keeping is one way to resist the evils of the present age, which he identifies as insatiable and misdirected desire promulgated by the values and images of market capitalism. For Owens, Sabbath keeping is a form of resistance to the desires of the market for more consumers and the reformation of our desires toward greater love of God and neighbor. He is particularly critical of the ways in which Sabbath keeping is marketed as merely a balm for weary souls instead of "challenging capitalism's technologies of desire."[32] He writes:

31. See Bass, "Keeping Sabbath"; Dawn, *Sense of the Call*; Heschel, *Sabbath*; Owens, "Sabbath-Keeping"; Wirzba, *Living the Sabbath*; and O'Flaherty and Peterson, *Sunday, Sabbath, and the Weekend*.

32. Owens, "Sabbath-Keeping," 205–6. I am always uncomfortable with unqualified critiques of capitalism given the ways in which my own vocation is supported by the resources available for teaching and research by those who have found various degrees of financial success in a capitalist market. Rasmussen, in *Moral Fragments and Moral Community*, makes a very helpful distinction between a market economy and a market society in chapter 6, "Market and State as Moral Proxies." While a capitalist market *may* result in the fair distribution of goods and services, it is morally problematic when all goods necessary for human flourishing become subject to market principles, even religion.

In fact, it is much to the market's advantage for workers and consumers to get a little rest, especially if it is "spiritual" rest, for the market does not care how we *feel*, it just wants our bodies . . . In this respect, Sabbath-keeping has been reduced to one more expression of popular, marketable spirituality. The vast majority of spiritualities on the market today collude with capitalism; they are balms the market offers to help us ease our consciences about giving the market our bodies to do with them as it likes. This is not surprising. What is sad and surprising is that so robust and ancient a practice as Sabbath-keeping can be co-opted to help the market keep our lives in bondage.[33]

Sabbath keeping as a practice is a form of resistance that helps us establish different patterns that reflect our loyalties to God and our concern for others. For Owens, it is a time for freeing ourselves from producing and shopping, for engaging in works of mercy and charity, and for being fully present in order to worship and celebrate the Lord's Day with the people of God.

I have begun to experiment with Sabbath keeping by establishing new patterns as a form of resistance to what normally consumes my days. I realize that as a person of privilege—one who has great autonomy over her schedule, enormous flexibility in managing her workload, and a more than sufficient income—I can experiment with Sabbath keeping. I remain disturbed that I have the privilege of Sabbath keeping, because there are countless persons in the service industries who work around the clock to support the workings of our economy by which I benefit.[34] This practice has heightened my moral sensibilities (I hope) that extend Sabbath keeping beyond providing some kind of inward peaceful benefit for myself into a concern for justice for others in work, wage earning, and time off for rest, as a way of resisting the power of the market for determining human worth and value. I have resisted turning on my computer to push against the intrusion of work into Sabbath-time, and the pathological need to always be in touch based on an inflated sense of self-importance. I have

33. Owens, "Sabbath-Keeping," 206.

34. See Young, "Five Faces of Oppression," in *Justice and the Politics of Difference.* The five faces are exploitation, marginalization, powerlessness, cultural imperialism, and violence. I am especially indicted by Young's category of powerlessness in contrast to my vocational privileges of autonomy in managing and directing my own work, decision-making, use of time, position of authority, and opportunities to engage in reflection and leisure as opposed to the powerless, who have few or none of these benefits in employment.

organized online courses that I teach to open on Monday mornings and end on Saturdays at 6 p.m. to give students an opportunity to establish patterns that resist and reform the ways we conceive of our days, how we relate to our work, and how we manage time and responsibilities on the other six days of the week. I'm under no illusion that this practice can solve the many economic and environmental injustices in our world, but at least it is a start in reformulating our desires and paying attention to how our lives are so shaped and constrained by the forces around us. Practices have this vital function of establishing habits and patterns of resistance as important means for responding to God's desires for the world and for our participation in them in spiritually and morally forming ways.

Conclusion

Few Christians would argue that practices are not important to spiritual and moral formation. Yet spirituality and morality often are viewed compartmentally, with separate sets of concerns and aspirations, often with the result that spirituality is somewhat privileged as a higher order desire while ethical reflection receives less attention. However, given that both Christian morality and spirituality have their roots in the goodness of God, are shaped by ultimate desires for God and right things to desire, and have hugely important practical components, practices become even more important for understanding how spiritual and moral formation are interrelated processes for growing up into an increasing love of God and love for neighbor in demonstrable and tangible ways.

In order to make the connections between spirituality and morality more explicit, I turn to exploring actual practices, turning the tables a bit to offer new conceptual schemes. In chapter 4, I will suggest that prayer—often classified as a spiritual discipline—is also an ethical practice, and speaking out against wrong doing, which one may see as an ethical practice, is also a spiritual discipline. I will employ similar arguments in chapters 5 and 6 by connecting simplicity with consumption practices and confession with resistance. My aim is to offer concrete examples and possibilities for communities of faith interested in (re)integrating spirituality and morality, with a focus on desire for God and the things of God as guides for Christian spiritual and moral formation.

four

Prayer and Speaking Out

I HAD AN EPIPHANY about ten years ago. At the time, the United States was preparing to invade Iraq as the start to the war on terror. A terrible conflict loomed, with all of the ensuing complications, complexities, conundrums, and costs. Regardless of how one might view the legitimacy of this action, a Christian ought to feel unease on entering into situations of violent conflicts and the inevitable harm done to persons, communities, infrastructures, and the environment. I was attending a Sunday morning worship service as the airwaves filled with the news of the impending invasion. As was customary, the service included a pastoral prayer. What was striking to me, and hence epiphanic, was the lack of reference to what was about to happen. Absolutely no mention was made of the upcoming reality of a nation going to war. The prayers offered focused on supplications for the psycho-spiritual needs of congregants and on a pious appreciation for Jesus as our best friend who knows what we need and the hardships we experience. While I believe that prayer is all-encompassing and that God cares about every hair on our head, it is important to affirm that God cares about so much more. As the weeks continued and have now turned into years, prayer concerns are expanded a bit to encompass "our" troops in harm's way. Rarely is mention made of the people of Iraq and Afghanistan or the growing awareness of the plight of Christians who are attempting to provide an alternative witness to sectarian divisions and hostilities.[1]

What does this situation say about the moral concerns of Christians we hear verbalized in our prayers? While most Christians agree that prayer

1. See a recent interview on the PBS program *Religion and Ethics*, "Disappearing Christians of Iraq," at http://www.pbs.org/wnet/religionandethics/episodes/july-23-2010/disappearing-christians-of-iraq/6701/.

is essential and significant for growth in our relationship with the Triune God, prayer also is a significant practice for moral formation. It enables us to grow in our concerns for others as we pray for justice and become willing to be part of God's response to human need. I turn now to an exploration of how two practices connect spirituality and morality. In this chapter, I will explore prayer and speaking out as a form of solidarity with others. While prayer may be classically referred to as a spiritual discipline, I am interested in probing how prayer is also a morally formative practice that teaches us compassion. While speaking out may be viewed as an ethical practice, I want to suggest that it is also spiritually forming because of what it requires of us in the pursuit of justice and of the virtues of compassion and courage.

Practices of Prayer and Speaking Out

I remember earlier in my life when I was learning how to live as a Christian. I am grateful for growing up in church communities where I learned fundamental practices, from simply showing up for church to serving with the youth group and playing the piano for choir. However, I do not remember too much instruction on how to pray. What I do remember is the suggestion that even if we don't feel like praying we should pray. While often simplistic in its antidote to perhaps more significant theological and pastoral issues, this early admonition does hold a clue for how to conceive of prayer as a practice that spiritually and morally shapes us. An overemphasis on a particular moment or feeling of what we might be inclined to do or not do can prevent us from actually doing something. This is where habits and practices play an important part in formation. Habits help us push through moments when our immediate proclivities actually prod us in an opposite, more negative direction. Small steps and risks do matter for longer-term purposes. Prayer for many of us is often this way. We pray even when we don't feel like it because there is something inherently good in the practice in spite of us.

Prayer is a crucial practice for faithful Christian living. Speaking out for others in an act of solidarity is an important moral mandate for the doing of justice and for paying attention to the "least of these"—those silenced, ignored, and living on the margins of our various communities.[2] What do prayer and speaking out have to do with learning to desire what

2. See the following two sources: Groff, "Just Praying, Acting Justly," and Johnson, "Praying: Poverty."

God desires? What do they do to foster desire for God and the things of God? How might prayer and speaking out be connected as spiritual and moral practices? How do they train us to focus on others and respond to others as part of our response to God? What kinds of dispositions and habits do prayer and speaking out require of us?

Desire for God and the Things of God

In its most basic and yet most profound way, prayer is a central means by which we communicate with God by offering our thanks and gratitude for who God is and what God has done, and for hearing from God in order to respond. Prayer takes place in a variety of ways and through a variety of forms: thanksgiving, supplication, confession, and intercession.[3] Prayer takes place in a variety of places: in solitude and in communities of faith, in worship, where two or three gathered, while driving, walking, or hiking, in planned times and in spontaneous outbursts of gratitude, and in cries for help. Prayer is not only the means by which we say something to God; it is also a means by which God communicates to us by directing our thoughts, reorienting our perspectives, responding to our real needs (as opposed to momentary wants), and heightening our awareness of God's presence and work in our lives. As Billy and Keating write, "Prayer itself is a human action made possible by the movement of God's grace in our lives. It embraces every dimension of our anthropological makeup—the physical, the emotional, the mental, the spiritual, and the social—and, as such, serves three important functions: the teleological, the instrumental, and the anthropological."[4] Prayer directs our attention to God's ends and, in doing so, helps us order our desires accordingly. Prayer serves the important purpose of hearing God. In this hearing is implied a discerning response to God through some kind of action incumbent upon us. Prayer encompasses the totality of human existence. There is no aspect of creation that does not concern God.

Prayer, especially when guided by Scripture and with eyes open to the needs around us, helps us gain clarity about what God desires for our lives and for all of creation.[5] Prayer is a means for discerning God's desires and

3. See the following two sources for rich insights on prayer: Foster, *Prayer*, and Saliers, *Soul in Paraphrase.*

4. Billy and Keating, *Conscience and Prayer*, 33–34.

5. Matthew Williams, a graduate of Ashland Seminary and associate pastor at

being willing to hear what they might be and how we might respond. According to Groody, prayer is a fundamental act of trust in God. He writes:

> Prayer is the doorway to self-knowledge, and it gives us a place to listen to God speaking to us in the depths of our hearts, in the events of our daily lives and in the contemporary world, and in the Scriptures. . . . [P]art of this exercise of trust involves identifying and cultivating "holy desires" that God inspires within us. Desires for forgiveness, justice in the world, peace of mind, a sense of mission, guidance in decisions, a renewed spirit, and help for loved ones are concrete ways in which we invite the Spirit of God to complete God's work within us.[6]

Prayer does not just cultivate desire for God. It also helps us gain clarity about what it is that God desires for our lives and for creation. This is an important dimension for those who profess to pray in Jesus' name, as Foster notes. Those who pray in Jesus' name do so as ones who desire conformity to Jesus and his ways, and for the purpose of realizing God's ends for human life.[7] Praying in Jesus' name assumes we will pray according to what Jesus desires and how Jesus might respond to the human needs around us. The Scriptures are replete with prayers of God's people, requesting such things as wisdom, mercy, knowledge, growth, compassion, and love. The imprecatory psalms cry out against injustice and wrongdoing, pleading with God to respond to remedy the situation. Prayers for deliverance and trust in God's rescue abound and are central for the lives of God's people. Prayers for such things as perseverance, faith, hope, understanding, and abounding love make possible faithful Christian living and holy communities. The content of our prayers reveals something about what concerns us and what we desire. It is important *that* we pray, of course, but in order for prayer to be spiritually and morally forming, it matters also *what* we pray since "prayer inspires and structures human life so that it becomes faithful

---

Ashland Brethren in Christ Church, read this chapter and offered significant suggestions. Of particular note is his reminder of how hermeneutics relates to our reading and use of Scripture, which will affect what we perceive to be God's desires for creation and hence for what we pray. He noted, "Yes, but different interpretations of Scripture can lead to several different trajectories of God's desires . . . consider the overly exuberant Patriot-Christian, or the anti-homosexual Christian . . . how does prayer shape us and the world even when we pray for things going against the grain of God's desires?" A great comment and a provocative question.

6. Groody, *Globalization, Spirituality, and Justice*, 251.

7. Foster, *Prayer*, 195.

and true."[8] Prayer helps order our desires and feed our affections. In attending to what we pray for, we are shaped to be more aware of and attentive to the needs around us. In this way, prayer is both a means of hearing God and of voicing our concerns for others by speaking out in prayer and in public.

In prayer we voice our concerns to God and call on God to help us respond in holy and just ways. In speaking out in our communities, we express our concerns for others, asking others to respond in holy and just ways. Just as prayer heightens our awareness of God's desires and reveals our shortcomings and failures in pursuing what God desires, so too does speaking out. In giving voice to the wrongdoing and wayward ways of our various communities, speaking out heightens our awareness of how our actions and attitudes harm others. This act of speaking out can also be understood as an act of solidarity, which recognizes our mutual connections and our responsibilities for others (and theirs for us). Solidarity is a concrete expression that makes public the things that God desires for our communities in such acts as speaking out and holding forth a higher and more just vision of our common life. Solidarity is where we stand—and the stands we take in actively paying attention to what is going on in our communities—and being willing to address concerns, wrongdoings, and injustices.

While prayer signals our trust in God, solidarity indicates our commitments and loyalties to God. According to Spohn, "Solidarity challenges any tendency to establish our relational identity by identifying exclusively with a finite community."[9] Our institutions and communities can be all-demanding of us. We are beholden to them in many ways: for salaries and benefits, for various privileges, for safety and protection, and for status and recognition. Spohn's concern relates to the ways in which communities can become idols. They can become places that attempt to usurp God's place by asking of us things that only God has the right to ask. We can be so easily blinded to the potentially harmful and destructive ideologies, policies, and practices within our institutions. Our unexamined allegiances to our communities can cause us to overlook their failings and shortcomings, and even to accept all that our institutions stand for and do as good. Speaking out against the very institutions of which we are part can become difficult, as those who dare to identify problems and harms are seen as dissenters and troublemakers, as disloyal. For example, I have been in many a faculty meeting over the years at various institutions where difficult and necessary

8. Benson and Wirzba, "Introduction," 2.

9. Spohn, *Go and Do Likewise*, 180.

conversations have taken place. Often the ethos, the goods and missional purposes of these institutions were at stake in these conversations. Decisions were often questioned and challenged, especially those made in secret or outside established, agreed-upon processes, while new proposals for possibilities were offered or rejected. Over the years, I have observed two things related to speaking out in public contexts. The first is how few dare to do it, even tenured faculty. The second is the likelihood of the same people speaking out, tending to exacerbate perceptions of those who are troublemakers and dissenters, those who dare to raise concerns and questions. I cannot count how many times my colleagues who remained silent, once the meeting was over, in private hallway conversations or behind closed office doors, expressed appreciation for and agreement with those who spoke out for the good of others. And I have stopped counting the number of times I have responded, "Then why didn't *you* say something?"

Speaking out as an act of solidarity may be difficult in contexts that understand moral agency in strictly individual terms and leave institutions and communities outside the bounds of moral critique.[10] It is also difficult when we might be privileged by a set of institutional arrangements that reinforces our status and security. Questioning these arrangements might deprivilege us and allow others to enjoy the benefits and privileges we assume to be exclusively ours. The motivation, therefore, to take a different stance on the politics, policies, and practices of our institutions may be low. An ethic of solidarity challenges us to examine and question the moral qualities of our communities, institutional practices, and relational arrangements with an eye to how the poor and voiceless are impacted and excluded. Solidarity presses us to take a position in our communities other than the one that preserves our privilege. Instead of working hard to maintain and defend our status, we use our voices (and, yes, our status and privilege) to speak out for others.

We speak out for the good of our communities, especially those that purport to exist for fulfilling an aspect of God's mission for the world. We ought to call ourselves to be and do better in our pursuit of justice by attending to concrete practices that facilitate good and human flourishing. While prayer enables us to better discern God's desires, speaking out for others enables God's desires to become visible and audible. For John Shea, prayer is a strategy for hope and justice in the world, an act of solidarity with others. He writes that in prayer,

10. See Strum, "Resisting Individualism, Advocating Solidarity."

the divine and the human are inseparably linked, and the bonds between people strengthened. The first line of the Lord's Prayer is, "Our Father in heaven." Although prayer may be an action of the solitary self, it always addresses the reality that binds people together. The opening word must be "our." If it is not, we are in danger of creating a private God, one who looks after us but is neglectful of others. Prayer would then foster division because some would have God and some would not. But, the God encountered in Christian prayer is the grounding of human solidarity.[11]

Prayer and speaking out require discernment of God's desires, commitments to embody the right things to desire, and the courage to pursue them in word and deed. Prayer is a moral practice as well as a spiritual discipline. Speaking out is a spiritual discipline as well an ethical action. The two reflect the interrelated elements of Christian spirituality and morality by a focus on others, a concern with dispositions and actions, with essential corporate and embodied dimensions.

Focus on the Good of Others

A classic form of prayer in which spiritual and moral dimensions most overtly occur is intercessory prayer, which Foster describes as a form of prayer that shifts "our center of gravity from our own needs to the needs and concerns of others."[12] In intercessory prayer, the focus is taken off of ourselves and redirected to the needs of others. It is an act of "kenosis" and "incarnation" in that we set aside the demand for our rights and needs to be met and we enter into the experiences of others.[13] It's important to note at this point that I am not advocating ignoring our personal needs and petitions before God. Nor am I encouraging prayer as a form of denial that minimizes ourselves in negative and dangerous ways in order to focus on the needs of others. This is a particularly important caution for women, who in our Christian communities might be socialized to practice a form of self-denial that actually robs us of agency and may even put our own lives at risk.[14] Our needs and concerns are important to God. As daughters

11. Shea, "Jesus' Response to God as Abba," 56.

12. Foster, *Prayer*, 191.

13. Mensch, "Prayer as Kenosis," 69–71.

14. While I appreciate the recovery of care as a moral criterion in ethics—prompted by works such as Gilligan's *In a Different Voice* and Nel Noddings' *Caring*—I am cautious

and sons of God, we can bring our concerns boldly before God with the expectation that God will respond. However, for prayer to be both morally and spiritually forming, our prayers must be directed and informed by the desires of God and a willingness to be shaped by what God desires for human life. Instead of finding a balance between praying for our own needs and interceding for the needs of others, perhaps we might see in prayer two important aspects crucial for moral formation. One is that in praying for the good of others, we are also praying for the good of ourselves, since the well-being of all creation is interrelated in significant ways. This enables us to let go of an inordinate amount of attention on ourselves in prayer in the hope that as others are praying for God's justice and mercy, our fundamental human needs will be met as God responds to their petitions. Two, in interceding for others we are giving voice for those whose voices tend to be silenced because of invisibility, distance, and indifference. Saliers writes that intercessory prayer

> requires looking clearly and truthfully at the world of humankind as it is, being aware of suffering and of the theater of conflicting passions. In interceding for the world and for others, we identify with others and enter into the capacity to bear their burdens. . . . [P]rayer as a corporate act of intercession holds the world in all its actuality up to God. In this sense it is a "worldy" activity. It is strenuous because it brings us to truthful perception of the world and of ourselves. Genuine intercessory prayer arouses and sustains the affective kinship with all who suffer. In it we are profoundly affected by the sense of solidarity with the whole race.[15]

Prayer requires of us a willing attentiveness to how others in our communities and world are affected by such things as violence, economic instability, unfair practices, discrimination, natural disasters, political instability, environmental destruction, tyranny, and oppression. Intercessory prayer puts before God and other hearers the good and well-being of persons,

---

in that an ethic of care is often assigned to women *because we are women* who tend to be socialized in order to care for the needs of others. These theories may exacerbate an unhealthy form of self-denial for women, especially in Christian contexts, which denies our moral agency, our needs, and our rights as meaning is ascribe to us primarily *through* male others. For helpful theological and moral perspectives on how Christian traditions may foster this unhealthy and risky aspect of self-denial in women, see the following: Albrecht, *Character of Our Communities*; Andolsen, "Agape in Feminist Ethics"; Crysdale, *Embracing Travail*; Hess, *Caretakers of Our Common House*; and Plaskow, *Sex, Sin, and Grace*.

15. Saliers, *Soul in Paraphrase*, 39.

believing that God is just as concerned about them as God is about us. Prayer draws us outward, and in doing so, it draws us into greater intimacy with those with whom and for whom we pray, perhaps even prompting us to act as an answer to prayer.

If we see intercessory prayer as a form of speaking out for others, the connections with speaking out as an act of solidarity become clearer. Speaking out for others in public forums is a way of making visible what might be invisible, ignored, forgotten, or unseen in our contexts. It focuses on the good of others and appeals to hearers that the impact of our decisions and actions on others be noticed and taken seriously. It lifts up God's desires for justice and contributes to speaking this kind of justice into existence in our communities by interceding for those whose life circumstances are constrained by our unjust and uncaring actions.

Saliers notes this interrelatedness of prayer and solidarity. He suggests four morally forming aspects of intercessory prayer.[16] First, prayer forces us to recognize our relationships with and dependence on others. Prayer puts us in relationship with God and with others, making us both vulnerable in our openness to God and others and more empathetic with God's concerns and the needs of others. Second, intercessory prayer disposes us toward compassion and solidarity, in that we stand with others as we stand up for others in acts of compassion and justice. Third, "we gain moral intentionality in addressing the world to God."[17] Prayer and solidarity force us to gain greater moral clarity about God's desires and how they should order our desires in response to the needs of others. While prayer is often necessarily spontaneous, prayer and solidarity also require moral intelligibility that undergirds our intercessions in prayer and in public, which is the fourth aspect of how prayer and solidarity are related. Saliers writes that "intercessory forms of prayer force us to recognize that religious faith must be lived in the world of power, conflicting passions and moral ambiguity. In our age and cultural circumstances prayer as praise must be connected with prayer as love of neighbor."[18] Intercessory prayer and speaking out for others are forms of love of neighbor and of God, the two great and interrelated commandments of Scripture. Prayer helps us gain a sharper perception of what God desires, and solidarity helps us vocalize and visualize God's desires in our communities.

16. Saliers, "Liturgy and Ethics," 29–30.
17. Ibid., 29.
18. Ibid., 30.

Dispositions and Actions: The Virtues of Compassion and Courage

If prayer and speaking out are informed by God's desires for justice and mercy, then they require the virtues of compassion and courage. Compassion and courage are needed for prayer and speaking out, but speaking out and prayer also become means by which we are formed to become more compassionate and courageous as we take steps toward embodying the desires of God.

Compassion literally means to "feel with" someone by sharing in their struggles in active ways. Spohn defines compassion as "the most active and engaged form of empathy, namely that disposition directed particularly to those in great need or suffering."[19] While empathy enables us to identify and enter into the experiences of others, compassion motivates empathy by moving us to action. Compassion is not an abstract feeling but a relational one, capable of stirring us to respond to human need. As a virtue, compassion is not just an inner disposition of sympathy for the plight of another. It is something we do in expressing our concern, outrage, and alarm at the sources and conditions of another's suffering. This causes us to speak out both in prayer and in public for the purpose of raising awareness, motivating response, and facilitating change. Practicing intercessory prayer teaches and disposes us toward compassion because it forces us to be more aware of others and what is going on around us, and to name these concerns before God and others. In this act of naming, we take on degrees of responsibility for addressing these concerns. Compassion requires moral perception— what Spohn identifies as "the active ability to grasp the human significance of a situation, to be receptive to its significance for benefiting or harming people."[20] Prayer is not a form of escape from the cares of the world but a practice that makes faithful living in the world more possible. Living faithfully in the world and fulfilling God's desires requires compassion because God is compassionate, the One who "feels with us" and is disposed to act justly and with mercy on our behalf.

Compassion as a virtue needs to be taught and modeled in our faith communities. Prayer becomes an important means by which we learn how to listen to God, how to listen to others, how to be in relational proximity to others' concerns, and how to pray accordingly. While prayer helps us discern God's desires and enables us to enter into the experiences of others

19. Spohn, *Go and Do Likewise*, 90.
20. Ibid., 93.

by interceding for them, developing compassion as a virtue also requires action. Roberts writes that "even though if I do not feel very compassionate at any given moment, I may still be in a position to say a kind word, lend a hand, or make some gesture of solidarity. And if I do, it's a good chance that felt compassion will not be long in coming."[21] Three things may ensue from simply starting to pray for others and practicing compassion, or even witnessing those who do. We begin to see ourselves in solidarity with others. We are drawn into relationship with others, and we take on their concerns. Compassion deepens in the context of relational solidarity as we continually feel with and act for others.[22] Compassion is developed and learned through paying attention to what is going on in the world, and by interceding with God and with others in our faith communities for those harmed and oppressed. We intercede on behalf of the multiple ways in which God's desires for justice and mercy fail to be acknowledged and lived out in the world. Often this intercession must take place in public forums by speaking out for others.

As compassion draws us to see the needs of others, courage enables us to speak out in the face of risks, dangers, threats, and harms. Courage is the mental, physical, psychological, and spiritual fortitude to confront and withstand fear, risks, threats, and dangers. Courage is one of the four cardinal virtues in Greek philosophy, along with temperance, wisdom, and justice. Courage is a virtue that helps us find the middle ground between cowardice and unwise foolhardiness in rushing in and acting without thought.[23] We should neither remain silent in the face of harm nor act blindly, unthinkingly, when the threats are great. As a moral virtue, courage requires seeing what confronts us and recognizing the risks involved to others and ourselves, and acting wisely in spite of the risks. Our moral fortitude is not only a personal disposition but also a necessary social virtue in our institutional contexts and in our global world.

Psychologist Gerd Meyer describes the need for social courage as a public virtue given the challenges of globalization, the demonization of difference, and prevailing injustice in targeting specific groups for ill treatment.[24] He defines social courage as a "specific form of courageous

21. Roberts, *Spiritual Emotions*, 196.

22. Ibid., 196.

23. See my discussion on Aristotelian virtue ethics in my *Reviving Evangelical Ethics*, 51–61.

24. Meyer, "Taking Risks for Others," 82. See also the collection of essays in Pury and Lopez, *Psychology of Courage*.

72

action—not just for myself (e.g., a bungee jump), but towards others and in public."[25] According to Meyer, social courage is needed in a variety of situations, such as when the rights of a person or group are violated and, due to an imbalance of power, no process exists by which to address such violations. He distinguishes social courage from a more generalized notion of courage as fortitude by the particularities of a given situation requiring specific kinds of actions. He writes:

> ... it is the *specific character of the situations* where it [social cour-age] is in demand: there is a conflict, an imbalance of power, risks, or possible disadvantages, and interactions are public. Social cour-age is not limited to acute or single situations ("emergencies") that unexpectedly require immediate action. Often, but not always, there is a "perpetrator" and a "victim." It may also include situ-ations in which dissatisfaction and pressure to act increase over time; e.g., on the job, in institutions, or in the community. If some-one wants to act courageously in these situations, he or she usu-ally waits for the "right moment and the right place" to articulate himself or herself, alone or supported by others.[26]

This "right moment and right place" courageous acting requires wis-dom and discernment, the ability to know not just what to do but how and when. Social courage, according to Meyer, may take the form of spontane-ous intervention when one witnesses a wrong being done; standing up for values and ideals, for other person's rights in organizations; and defending one's self and others against injustice, attacks, and pressures to act wrongly by saying no.[27]

While he writes for a European context (Germany) confronting its particular challenges, Meyer's insights are pertinent for understanding how courage might be publically expressed in a variety of contexts, especially when there are shared uncertainties about status and privilege, economic and political instabilities, threats perceived or real, and where pressures to conform and keep silent about injustice might be exceptionally strong. Of particular relevance to the relationship between becoming a wise moral ac-tor and navigating complex moral contexts, a key ingredient of moral for-mation, are Meyer's insights on what kind of person may be more inclined to act courageously. While Meyer discovered a variety of factors, the one

25. Meyer, "Taking Risks for Others," 84.
26. Ibid., 85. Italics in original.
27. Ibid., 85–88.

most interesting for the relationships between compassion and courage is the ability to "pay attention and to show concern for what happens to others, to feel at least partly responsible, and the readiness to act accordingly."[28] This requires proximity to others in order for empathy and compassion to form and for responsibility to take shape, as well as dispositions and proclivities to act ethically if social courage is to become moral action.[29] According to Meyer, values and principles must be learned and internalized; moral beliefs must come from deeply rooted affections; and there must be an ever present readiness to take responsibility for others based on care.[30]

Crucial for developing these capacities for social courage are the kinds of moral values that orient persons and motivate us to act on behalf of others. Important for social courage are compassion and empathy as motivating feelings and "wisdom-in-situation."[31] Not to be ignored, according to Meyer, are the contexts that help shape us to act one way or another. Communities that require and even demand conformity will likely aid in shaping persons to accept the norms of the group, with little regard for the moral implications. In fact, the moral norm in such situations may be to simply accept and conform, whereas challenging and questioning are cast as moral violations. Meyer also notes the important role of leadership and how leaders may form a cultural ethos that seeks to reward truth telling and social courage as opposed to scapegoating and penalizing those who speak out. Sadly, he is not optimistic about the value of social courage, given the ways in which people and institutions tenaciously hang onto power and privilege. Yet courage is a crucial virtue needed for establishing and maintaining communities of justice who responsibly and compassionately care for others.

Prayer and speaking out are practices that form us in a variety of ways. They require similar dispositions and actions, most notably courage and compassion. They are means of expressing God's desires, and as such, they somehow bring these desires into being through our intercessions in prayer and public. They are also practices of hope; we believe that praying and speaking out do make a difference in our world. Prayer and speaking out are elements of a fully Christian life where spirituality and morality are

28. Ibid., 92.

29. Ibid., 95.

30. Ibid.

31. See the important discussion on wisdom by van der Ven in *Formation of the Moral Self*, 77.

intertwined in our desire for God and the things of God. As Richard Gula writes:

> Petitions and intercessions are not for passive souls. These prayers are not attempts to escape social responsibility by turning over to God what we want nothing to do with. Rather, prayers of faith and trust lead us toward God in love and gratitude and, in so doing, they also lead us toward the loving service that expresses our interdependence with others and creation. To pray with the formula "in and through Christ" is to pray through the whole body of Christ, which includes us. Remember, God comes to us through us. This is the way of the incarnation. So in our petitions and intercessions, we are doing more than asking God to intervene. We are also committing ourselves to assume responsibility to bring about that for which we pray. That is to say, our prayers have a self-involving character to them, which is the inner dynamic of determination. This is not just the determination of shamelessly persisting in our petition, it is even more the determination to live into that for which we pray.[32]

Embodied Spirituality and Morality: Possibilities for Practices

How might prayer and speaking out be embodied and practiced so that they form us and become a natural part of who we are and what we do? One of the great gifts of Christian faith is Christian community and the witness of many faithful practitioners who offer us courage and examples for speaking out and prayer that embody God's desires, shape our own, and enable us to respond to human need and continue our work for justice. I end this chapter by introducing some of these witnesses and offering suggestions for prayer as a moral practice and speaking out as a spiritual discipline. My descriptions of these examples and suggestions will be somewhat brief; my hope is that they pique our curiosities enough to explore them on our own and experiment in finding ways to bring prayer and speaking out together in our Christian formation.

Stassen and Gushee observe that "it is hard to think of a more neglected issue in Christian ethics than prayer" even though Jesus offers us instructions on practices of prayer.[33] Prayer was practiced by Jesus and is part of working for the kingdom of God to be realized in our lives on earth

---

32. Gula, *Call to Holiness*, 165.
33. Stassen and Gushee, *Kingdom Ethics*, 499.

even as we await its consummation. Jesus offers us a model of prayer and specific instructions on how and what to pray that balance what we need with what others need in light of God's kingdom (Matt 5:7–13). While the gospels portray Jesus seeking solitude in order to pray, a practice crucial for Jesus' faithful fulfillment of God's calling, the gospels do not indicate that Jesus privileged prayer and solitude above other aspects of a life with God. He preached, healed, taught, and spoke against the harms humans do to each other. As Stassen and Gushee note, Jesus cautions against the kinds of prayers that are overly focused on demonstrating one's own self-righteousness while ignoring the righteousness that comes from God.[34] In the gospels, Jesus' own prayers are drawn outward to God and in concern for others. Even his haunting prayer before his execution was the desire to do the will of God on behalf of his mission and calling from God, which eventually led to his death. Jesus' searches for times of solitude and prayer were often accompanied by actions in his ministry where he was filled with compassion, where he spoke truth to others, and where he acted on behalf of others. In Jesus' life we see the dynamic interplay between prayer as a way of hearing and prayer as a way of being encouraged to do the will of God. Saliers writes, "Christ's own life is one of active prayer and prayerful action. It is fitting to speak of his whole life as a prayer, a continual self-offering to the Father. In exploring what Christ's life signifies we are led to ponder anew the necessity of understanding prayer and action not in opposition, but in tension required by particular moments in that stream of life which seeks to grow into the full stature of Christ."[35]

Christian formation leading to spiritual and moral maturity involves both prayer and action. Based on the example of Jesus, we first start by challenging the divide between prayer and action by locating prayer as a form of action before God on behalf of others and action as a form of prayer that seeks to call into existence God's will for human flourishing.

Reading Scripture with an attention to its larger social contexts is also a way to integrate prayer with action. Some of us have perhaps been raised in contexts that value the Bible as a personal devotional book. While this may be one way in which God speaks to us through Scripture, it misses the larger dimensions of Scripture, namely, the economic, political, and social contexts in which it was written and given. Scripture was not written in a vacuum. This occurred to me again as I was reading Exodus, intrigued

34. Ibid., 450–53.

35. Saliers, *Soul in Paraphrase*, 101.

by all that was going on in the earlier chapters of Israel's enslavement in Egypt, Pharaoh's power, and the back and forth between Moses, Pharaoh, and court officials. As our liberation theologians remind us, this context is important for understanding the desire for freedom to serve God alone, the hegemonic power exercised in keeping a group of people enslaved for the benefit of others, and the ways in which despots ignore the impact of their tyranny on the lives of others. Part of Scripture's power is what it shows us about the world in which we live and how it might guide us in prayer against the powers and principalities of our world. Madame Guyon introduced us to the practice of "praying the Scripture."[36] Perhaps this discipline can be formative as we allow Scripture to direct us to the contexts and realities that govern people's lives, such as oppression, enslavement, abusive political leaders, economic hardships, mass migrations, violence, famine, and fleeing and living as refugees. As I was rereading Exodus while writing this chapter, I found myself drawn to pray for (and against) modern-day Pharaohs and currently enslaved and oppressed people. Scripture itself, when read with a commitment to understanding God's desires for creation, can help us combine prayer with action on behalf of others.

Using guides can also help us appreciate prayer's morally forming dimensions. My friend and colleague David deSilva suggests that one such helpful guide is the *Book of Common Prayer*. In particular, "prayers of the people" are means of intercession that offer "many focal points so that we can pray in line with the breadth of Scripture's whole vision for prayer and not allow our prayer lives to be distorted by focusing on some small part of this vision."[37] Prayers that direct us outward—a fundamental movement of spiritual and moral formation—can help us see the needs and concerns around us as just as important as our own. DeSilva notes that a practice of prayer that intentionally focuses on others is a much needed one given pastoral prayers (such as the situation I described at the beginning of this chapter) that "too frequently remain entirely focused on the present congregation in the present moment, contributing to the congregation's inner-directed, self-centered focus rather than challenging them to expand their scope of concern beyond their walls."[38] Prayer as a means of moral and spiritual formation *must* be intentional. It requires not just openness to God and willingness to hear but also knowledge about what God cares

---

36. Guyon, *Experiencing the Depths of Jesus Christ*.

37. deSilva, *Sacramental Life*, 124.

38. Ibid., 125.

about and what is going on in the world. The famous dictum "read the Bible in one hand and the newspaper in the other," purportedly coined by Karl Barth, is important for praying with eyes wide open to the events of the world. Prayer is not a means of escape but instead a way of confronting the chaos, injustice, and evil of the world by interceding with God on behalf of others. I find myself using this phrase as I pray: "Lord, as your Spirit hovered over the chaos in creation, bringing a just order, hover now over your creation, in all the places [here I name them] of chaos and disorder, and bring a just peace."

One of my favorite examples of a rich combination of prayer and speaking out is Walter Rauschenbush's *Prayers of the Social Awakening*.[39] Rauschenbush, a pastor and activist in the Hell's Kitchen area of New York in the late nineteenth and early twentieth centuries, left us a legacy of prayers for all sorts of things that raise concerns and voices those concerns to God and others: for street children, immigrants, service workers, political figures, wage earners, teachers, and many others. His prayers can be used and recontextualized for our contexts by giving voice to contemporary concerns.[40] Another rich example of how prayer becomes a means of speaking out is the collection of prayers, *Conversations with God: Two Centuries of Prayers by African Americans*.[41] In the experiences of slavery, oppression, violence, and discrimination, prayers become means for speaking out and for solidarity with all others, even for oppressors and violent ones. The book *Resist: Christian Dissent for the Twenty-First Century* contains powerful prayers that embolden us to be courageous, take risks, and resist those things that work against God's love and justice for creation.[42] One of my favorites is the "Prayer for the Courage to Resist" by Alison Boden, by which we ask God to help us resist the temptation to hoard resources, as well as evil policies and social structures, and seek help in speaking truth to power and working for justice and reconciliation.[43] The prayers offered by others can be prayed by us and used a means in our own faith communities

39. Rauschenbusch, *Prayers of the Social Awakening*.

40. For a recent example, see Iosso and Hinson-Hasty, *Prayers for the New Social Awakening*.

41. Washington, ed., *Conversations with God*. I'm grateful that my friend and colleague, Rev. Dr. JoAnn Ford Watson, introduced me to this source.

42. Long, *Resist! Christian Dissent for the Twenty-First Century*.

43. Boden, "We Pray for the Courage to Resist," 59–61.

for drawing our attention to the realities of our world and how prayer might be a form of speaking out about them to our gracious God.

How might we support and participate in prayer and speaking out in our own contexts? Perhaps gathering with trusted friends and colleagues to pray for our institutions is a good start. Mustering up the courage to ask questions that get at deeper issues is a catalyst to speaking out. Minimizing the distance between persons in our institutions is important, too, especially for those of us who benefit from a particular professorial rank or tenure. How much do we know about the workloads and conditions of our support staff? How are they affected by the privileges extended to us that are not extended to them? How are they treated? How are they paid? Creating and maintaining friendships across ranks and positions help draw us closer to the lives of others, enabling care to become more relational, more compassionate, and more just as our awareness is heightened by the situations and contexts of others. We can support those who speak out by following up on their comments with affirmation and interest while issues are still on the table. And we take small steps in speaking out, using our voices. Who knows where these small steps may lead in the work of justice?

Conclusion

Prayer is part of morality and speaking out is part of spirituality. They are important practices in an unjust world that relies on those committed to what God desires to do the work that God requires. As Groody reminds us, "Prayer is not just a psychological tool for self-actualization but a spiritual grace that facilitates human transformation. It is a fundamental human need and is especially important for those involved in the work of justice. Prayer and justice are two sides of the same spiritual coin: justice without prayer quickly degenerates into frenetic social activism, but prayer without justice is hollow and empty."[44]

What do I say to that? Amen . . . May our prayers and speaking out be just, deep, and full, reflective of the desire for God and God's desires for our world.

---

44. Groody, *Globalization, Spirituality, and Justice,* 250.

five

Simplicity and Consumption of Resources

A FEW YEARS BACK in a theology course at Ashland Seminary, students were exploring the important relationships between our theological claims and moral commitments in reference to our care for creation and the use of natural and manufactured resources. Current environmental and ecological concerns and disproportionate rates of consumption around the globe raise important questions about the damages and effects of human practices on our shared spaces and goods in God's creation. The topic in class turned to practices. One student raised the question that perhaps others were also asking: "What difference can I make given the enormity and expansiveness of environmental concerns?" The recycling bin in his home was downstairs in an old house with creaky and narrow stairs. Taking a can or two, or other recyclable items downstairs, took more time than just throwing them away in the regular trash container. In hiking up and down the stairs to recycle, James thought to himself, "For every can I take downstairs, I know there are millions of recyclable items discarded in landfills, oceans, water supplies, and poor neighborhoods all over the globe. What difference does my one or two items really make?"

This led to a great discussion, as all honest and provocative questions should. Discussing our relationships to what we consume through the lenses of practices led us to this conclusion: These small, important steps of recycling do make a difference, not just because "every little bit helps." Every little bit does help. From the perspective of a formative practice, this often inconvenient one of recycling—and taking materials to a specific location if there is no city pickup—causes us to *think* about what we consume, what we are doing in our use of resources, and to examine our consumption practices. Our initial conclusions were that while we believe that recycling does make a difference to our environment, it also makes a difference in how we think about and order the spaces in which we live and the resources we consume.

This conversation from class with a great group of students offers a context for the concerns of this chapter, which are the relationships between simplicity and consumption habits that link Christian spirituality and morality. I will explore how simplicity and consumption relate to our desire for God and God's desire for our use of resources and care of shared spaces; how they are formative for us and for how they focus on the good of others; and how they might become means of helping us learn virtues of self-control and gratitude as important for Christian formation. I end with some suggestions for how simplicity and the just use of resources might be practiced in our various contexts.

Practices of Simplicity and Consumption

There has been a renewed interest in simple lifestyles as a result of the economic crises caused by the meltdown of the housing market and high unemployment rates, the shift from a manufacturing to a service economy, increasing prices of good and commodities, and the financial volatility and unpredictability of global markets. It seems this renewed interest has been caused by reduced incomes and fears of losing one's job or home. I have heard little reflection on how our consumption practices and our eschewing of more moderate means of living may have caused some of our financial difficulties in the first place. In the "fasting from buying clothes" suggestions popular over the last couple of years, the motivation seems to be the lack of space for new clothing items in already burgeoning closets. One individual, who vowed to fast for one month from buying new clothes, shoes, or accessories each time she walked into a store, expressed the desire to remove the fashion idol from her heart so that she might grow closer to God while saving the gift cards she received to spend after her month-long fast was over as a reward. Simplicity is seen as a reaction to our current economic messes, as a way of getting by in times of uncertainty as opposed to a valued practice, one worth doing simply because simple lifestyles might be good in and of themselves and foster good for others.

What is simplicity? In the context of Christian faith, simplicity is grounded in our belief in God as the One who provides what is necessary for us to live. It demands of us clarity and commitment to what we actually *need* as opposed to what we may *want*. Making this distinction is important for the choices we make for how we spend money, the kinds of houses and cars we buy, the amount of clothing and the number of shoes in our closets (ouch!), what we do with our time, and how we use all sorts of resources at our disposal. Daniel Groody offers this description of simplicity: "Simplicity is a practical way of trying to live more and more in harmony with the earth. As a lifestyle of responsible stewardship for God's creation, it is also an act of solidarity with those who come after us. Few lifestyles swim more upstream against the current of contemporary society than simplicity. In a world where we are consistently told that more is better, simplicity seeks to free us from the slavery of inordinate human want."[1]

Simplicity is informed by the theological claim that the earth and all that is in it belong to the Lord. God created the earth as sufficient to support human well-being and flourishing: food, clean air, healthy communities, meaningful work, shelter, and relational harmony between God and humans, humans with each other, and humans with the rest of creation. Humans are part of God's creation and placed in it in positions of responsible stewardship. There have been important critiques raised about the misunderstanding, misappropriation, and misuse of a human stewardship model of creation whereby dominion becomes understood as lordship, sovereignty, unbridled rights to control the earth's resources and the unrestrained use of them. According to Paul Santmire, Protestant conceptions of dominion are rooted in deeply anthropocentric understandings of the creation narratives in Genesis, which place humans at the apex of God's creation.[2] This birth order has been taken by humans to mean a privileged place in creation at the expense of all other creatures, including nature. Such things as animals, plants, mineral resources, and land are ascribed value only in ways that meet human needs, and are used in ways that ignore their own integrity as part of God's creation. For Santmire, this faulty theology of dominion can be corrected by reevaluating long-standing Protestant tenets. We need a new ecological paradigm that will demand significant revisions for how we think about and live in God's creation, and how we might understand our proper role. The two most salient Protestant claims for Santmire are *sola gratia* and *sola scriptura*. He writes that "with our vision enlightened by the ecological paradigm, the grace we can see is the life of God overflowing, predicated on self-giving love, to the whole creation,

---

1. Groody, *Globalization, Spirituality, and Justice*, 258.

2. Santmire, "Healing the Protestant Mind."

not primarily to the human creature. This promise proclaimed in Scripture can be heard not just as the gift of human salvation, but also as the gift of a new heavens and a new earth in which righteousness dwells for the sake of all creatures."[3]

For Santmire and other constructive theologians concerned with how theological systems have justified our poor treatment of the environment and unchecked use of resources, Scripture itself raises our awareness of God's relationship with, care of, and love for *all* creation. A renewed concern for creation must start with a more humble and modest understanding of our role within the created order, along with an appreciation of God's continual care for creation in anticipation of the new earth and new heavens. While humans may have been designated as the species that uniquely bears the image of God (Gen 1:27), humans are not the center of creation. God is the center. Yet, humans are created in the image of God in ways that no other creatures are. Terence Fretheim reminds us of the scriptural location of our disputed understandings of the *imago Dei* in the context of the creation narratives in Genesis 1. This context is one of God's creative activity so that the "human vocation to be in God's image . . . is to be modeled on the creative words and actions of God."[4] We image a particular God who deigned to share power with humans in order to be in genuine relationship with us. This is important for Fretheim, since the ways in which we respond to others is modeled on the ways in which God responds to us. Therefore, our images of dominion must be informed by how we understand God's charge to humans about our responsibilities. Fretheim writes, "The very first words that God speaks to the newly created human beings assume the gift of power and its (potential) exercise: be fruitful, multiply, fill the earth, have dominion, subdue the earth (1:28). Given the imaging of God we have discerned up to this point, these words of commission should be interpreted fundamentally in terms of *creative word and deed* and not domination or violence."[5]

In these commands, God shares power with human creatures, giving us a say in how the resources and goods of creation will be cared for in ways that reflect God's love and justice. This is the meaning of "subdue" in Genesis 1:28, according to Fretheim. In the context of the first creation narrative, subdue does not mean coercion and subjugation of nonhuman

3. Ibid., 69.

4. Fretheim, *God and World in the Old Testament*, 48.

5. Ibid., 49. Italics in original.

creatures for the sole purpose of meeting our needs. Instead, subdue is the task humans are given to work in God's creation, enabling it to become what God intends it to be by honoring the integrity and interdependence of all created life. Christopher Wright also explores the ways in which "subdue" and "have dominion" ought to be informed by how we understand God's relationship to and work in creation. Wright opts for an understanding of humanity's responsibility in and to creation as "servant-kingship" as opposed to the overly familiar concept of stewardship. Stewardship continues the focus on humans as somehow central and "in charge" of what God created, free to use what is at our disposal in ways we see fit. It tends to be reduced to the yearly stewardship campaigns at churches, with the more limited focus on money to the exclusion of how we relate to all of the earth's resources, as well connoting management as opposed to caring relationships.[6] For Wright, servant-kingship keeps our understanding of our responsibilities in and to creation in its proper theological and relational context, starting with God's own love for and relationship to all of creation. Therefore, "to rule over the rest of creation as king, to act as the image of God as King, is to do biblical justice in relation to non-human creation. To 'speak out for those who cannot speak,' is a task of human kingship that could as relevantly describe our responsibility toward the rest of creation as to the human subjects of a ruler."[7]

Humans were created to be dependent on God *and* interdependent on the right working of creation in which we have an integral role to play. This is the reality of *our* interdependence with God's creation. Without sufficient food, we will die. Without clean water, we become sick. Without healthy communities, we do not flourish. Without meaningful work, we are thrust to the margins of society. Without adequate resources, our lives are at risk. Both overconsumption and underconsumption are detrimental to creaturely existence. We need creation as creation needs us. Our care for creation must therefore extend to a refreshed view of how we are related to creation and how we ought to live *in* creation in light of our responsibilities to others and our use of shared and finite resources. Responsible stewardship of God's creation demands the wise, moderate, and purposeful use of

6. Wright, "Earth Is the Lord's," 230.

7. Ibid., 231. Of course, this depends on how we understand kingship, which Fretheim also addresses. While the creation narratives imply God's sovereignty, we must always bear in mind that God is a king like no other king in the ways in which God cares for and relates to creation, and shares power and responsibility with humanity. See *God and World in the Old Testament*, 46–48.

the earth's resources because we share this space with others. The place to start might be with simpler ways of living in light of our responsibilities to others and because of communal and limited resources.

While simplicity and care for creation may be obvious moral commitments in terms of the choices and commitments we make to pursue what is good for God's creation, embodied in such practices as consumption and recycling, what qualifies them as concerns of Christian spirituality? Our concern for creation and ways of living as responsible image-bearers are intricately connected with our faith in God; our desire for God and for the things of God, particularly in doing justice; and our perspective on the things we own and consume.

Desire for God and the Things of God

Simplicity is grounded in our ultimate desire for God and is guided by the command to seek "first for the kingdom of God and his righteousness" (Matt 6:33). We are to strive to possess and take hold of God's kingdom. This desire for God's kingdom shapes, modifies, and qualifies our desire for things we do possess so that we might be free to pursue the things that God desires. This notion of striving for God's kingdom is an aspect of simplicity that requires rightly ordered desires as key to spirituality, starting with our desire for God. We establish thoughtful priorities based on this ultimate desire that informs our actual practices in how and what we consume and possess. In his book *Freedom of Simplicity*, Foster writes that the kingdom of God refocuses our vision when it comes to understanding simplicity. He writes:

> We are to discipline ourselves to "seek *first* the kingdom of God." This focus must take precedence over absolutely everything. We must never allow anything, whether deed or desire, to have that place of central importance. The redistribution of the world's wealth cannot be central; the concern for ecology cannot be central; the desire to get out of the rat race cannot be central; the desire for simplicity itself cannot be central. The moment any of these becomes the focus of our concern, it has become idolatry. Only one thing is to be central: the kingdom of God. And, in fact, when the kingdom of God is genuinely placed first, the equitable

> distribution of wealth, ecological concerns, the poor, simplicity, and all things necessary will be given their proper attention.[8]

Foster locates simplicity as an inward discipline. While I am deeply appreciative of Foster's work and its enduring importance for more wholistic understandings and practices of Christian spirituality, the location of simplicity as an "inward" discipline may unintentionally create a bifurcation between spirituality and morality, a concern I have been addressing throughout this book. I have suggested that authentic spirituality is not (just) inward and interiorized but instead public and embodied with important social implications. So while Foster does hold a high regard for such things as the equitable distribution of wealth, ecological concerns, and care for the poor, he is not quite so clear as to what proper attention to them might entail as part of striving for God's kingdom *and* righteousness. There may be an inadvertent danger in once again privileging a kind of seeking for God's kingdom that remains inward and "merely" spiritual without the requisite attention to the ways in which our desire for God must be accompanied by the kind of righteousness and justice that God desires.

Might I suggest that by seeking or desiring the kingdom of God first, we must at the same time heighten our moral awareness about such issues as the equitable distribution of wealth, ecological concerns, and care for the poor? The command given by Jesus is to "strive first for the kingdom of God *and* his righteousness." Striving for God's kingdom and striving for God's righteousness go together in the command. On the surface, the link between spirituality and morality seems obvious: seeking God (a spiritual quest) and seeking righteousness (a moral one) are related, and things we are commanded to do. I think they are more intricately connected and do not exist in separate domains. Moral concerns are not simply results of seeking first God's kingdom but are part of the kingdom we are seeking as we make it our first priority with its call to a way of life that reflects the values and commitments of Jesus. The word for righteousness is *daikaiosunē*, which is also translated as "justice," reminding us that a commitment to justice is central to God's kingdom, and therefore central to our understandings of Christian spirituality and morality. We desire God and the things of God by pursuing, above all other desires, God's kingdom *and* the justice that so characterizes God's intentions for justice and righteousness.

The kingdom of God is all-encompassing in that there is not one aspect of our lives or in all creation that is outside the purview and care of

8. Foster, *Freedom of Simplicity*, 104–5. Italics in original.

God. While it may be popular and convenient to relegate our understanding of the kingdom of God to some future day, making it less demanding today, or to compartmentalize it as "only" a spiritual reality, even a cursory reading of the location of this command in the Sermon on the Mount will explicate the kinds of commitments and practices that kingdom people ought to pursue.[9] The command to "strive first" for God's kingdom and righteousness follows a series of sayings in Matthew 6 on how we are to relate to and think about possessions. We are to give generously what we have (6:1–4). We are to pray for *daily* bread (6:11). We are to refrain from hoarding and amassing treasures on earth (6:19–21). We are to resist the master that is mammon (6:24). We are to trust God and refrain from fretting about what we will eat or wear (6:25–32). As we practice these things that Jesus commands, we are to trust God and strive for, above all things, God's kingdom of justice. As we practice these things, we are embodying the kingdom of God. Our desires can be rightly ordered so that we might be free from the tangles of competing obligations and loyalties that tend to muddy and complexify our decisions and lifestyles. We can moderate and put into perspective our needs for clothing, food, and other necessities such as shelter and material resources. Yet, as we put them into proper perspective, we must be mindful that part of seeking God's kingdom requires the struggle for justice in God's creation so that all persons have what they need to survive and even thrive. This commitment to justice ought to modify our perspectives and practices on consumption of the goods we use and consume in light of our responsibilities to others.

It's important for me at this point to acknowledge how easy it is to fret less about material needs when my economic location and privilege assure that these needs will be met. My own class location and relational connections ensure modicums of safety nets that are often taken for granted. On one hand, it is more difficult to critique our "consumer society" since I benefit from it.[10] On the other hand, it is easy to criticize it as an "objective observer" when my basic necessities (and then some) are already being met. I have been shaped by our consumer society. The dangerous dimension of our consumer society, according to John Kavanaugh, is that it essentially shapes our desires for more, for better, and for newer—and in doing so, it shapes our values, our identities, and our practices. None of us is immune from its effects on our desires, what we think we need, and what

---

9. See Stassen and Gushee, *Kingdom Ethics*.

10. Kavanaugh, *Following Christ in a Consumer Society*, 4

we *must* have. Like Kavanaugh, Roger Owens also explores the pervasiveness of market capitalism for how it shapes insatiable desire when he writes: "Because human beings are desiring beings (and because, as Christians know, we have a tendency to desire *wrongly*), the market and its advertising gurus can step into the vacuum and train our desire to want insatiably."[11]

What is the impact of this insatiable consumption on our lives and on the lives of others? The statistics are staggering and sobering. We live in a country that consumes the majority of the world's shared resources. We are 5 percent of the world's population but consume 25 percent of the world's energy because of our bigger homes, bigger cars, lack of awareness, and reluctance to explore more efficient ways to share and use limited resources. We throw out 200,000 pounds of unused yet edible food each day while millions go hungry.[12] We are a nation where 70 percent of our economic activity is fueled by consumption. The amount of debt on credit cards—the easiest way to purchase whatever we want, whenever we want it—is enormous. The average debt carried on credit cards is $5,100 per holder; Americans charged $51 billion for fast food in 2006; and the total amount of *consumer* debt is $2.4 trillion, which averages to $7,800 per person.[13] Some credit card offers are marketed as forms of charity in that if the purchaser spends a certain amount, up to 1 percent will be donated to charity. In order to be charitable, we are stimulated to consume.

Even now, in the midst of our economic crises, much of the recovery rests in the hands of consumers, who have scaled back because of job insecurity, rising consumer debt, and the increasing prices of basic goods and services. Some of us just aren't buying, which is a *bad* thing for the global economy. I remember distinctly after the attacks of 9/11 that "consume" became a patriotic cry for unity in light of fears of market instability. We were asked to "go out and buy"—demonstrating very little recognition of how our inordinate consumption habits might contribute to global instability. Our desire for more (and cheaper) goods seeps farther and wider across the globe, threatening indigenous communities, access to land, and harming the environment as we search for always new and growing consumer markets and always cheaper ways to do business and buy stuff.

---

11. Owens, "Sabbath-Keeping," 204. Italics in original.

12. "Consumption: Industrialized, Commercialized, Dehumanized, and Deadly." Online: http://www.mindfully.org/Sustainability/Consumption-Industrialized-Commercialized.htm.

13. Zuliani, "Dozen Alarming Consumer Debt Statistics."

The tension this presents to Christian faith and practice was articulated well by one of my students, who was formed by the Mennonite tradition and who remains deeply rooted in its beliefs and practices. His family had made an intentional decision to live on one income—his wife's salary as a teacher—so that he could tend to the kids at home and serve a church as a pastor without draining the resources of this local congregation. He noted the irony of the conflict between his Christian commitments to live simply and the appeal made to consume more to keep the economy going, sensing his Christian lifestyle of reduced consumption was a cause of our economic crisis. Kevin experienced what Michelle Gonzalez describes in her book *Shopping*:

> Consumerism is an ideology. It promotes a value system that is staunchly against the core of Christian values. Consumerism values having and enjoying over serving, loving, and giving. Consumerism centers on ownership, on pleasure. When I see the word consumerism, the root "consume" jumps out at me. To consume is to devour. I liken it to eating. And no matter how much we eat, we always, inevitably, will get hungry again. And such is the case with material goods. Once we unleash our appetite for objects, we fall into a helpless cycle of consumption, satisfaction, and hunger.[14]

That most of us experience little conflict between our consumption patterns and our Christian faith is disturbing. In so many ways, the goal of the consumer society is to reinforce the belief that we are isolated individuals whose sole purpose in life is to pursue pleasure as opposed to rightly ordered desires. Consumerism relies on individuals to disregard wise shopping habits, ethical spending, and a more equitable use of resources. It does so by redirecting and reinforcing our focus on ourselves and shaping our desires to concentrate on our wants, with little regard to what we ought to desire for our lives. It is easy to see how this goes against the grain of Christian spirituality and morality, which has in view the impact of our decisions and behaviors on others.

Focus on the Good of Others

Christian spirituality and morality are other-centered. They flow from a desire for God and have in view the good of others. This is so true when it comes to the impact of our consumption choices on others. Our disordered

14. Gonzalez, *Shopping*, 13–14.

desires for "more of the latest" creates various disorders in the lives of others who are at the mercy of our consuming. What does consumption have to do with our desire for God and our concern for the good of others? *Everything*, according to William Cavanaugh. Consumerism itself is a "spiritual disposition" since it is "a way of looking at the world around us that is deeply formative."[15] Consuming becomes all-consuming of what we desire, who we are, how we connect with others, how we spend our time, and how we spend our money. This is indicting as I remember my own practices while on a weekend trip to visit my dear cousins. On my way to my cousin Denise's home, I just *had* to stop at an outlet just off the expressway, and then a supermarket to stock up on special food products that my husband and I enjoy. The result was a harried dinner because I was running late, and the shortening of our already short weekend visit by at least six hours.

We can be consumed by consuming. Instead of our desires being formed by the kingdom of God and the desire for justice, our desires are disordered and redirected to things that will ultimately never satisfy us. These disordered desires eventually harden our hearts and detach us from the people with whom we are connected. Cavanaugh writes:

> Most of us do not consciously choose to work others to death for the sake of lower prices on the things we buy. But we participate in such an economy because we are detached from the producers, the people who actually make our things. . . . The "happy meal" toys from McDonald's that we easily discard reveal nothing of the toil of the malnourished young women who make them. We spend the equivalent of two days' wages for such women on a cup of coffee for ourselves—without giving it a second thought. We do so not necessarily because we are greedy or indifferent to the suffering of others, but largely because those others are invisible to us.[16]

Invisible to us—but not invisible to the God who desires justice, mercy, humility, and wisdom in how we relate to others, how we use money, and how we free ourselves from conflicting loyalties to pursue God's kingdom and justice. Food, clothing, and shelter are critical for human existence and survival. Luxuries are not. Our desire for God and God's righteousness modifies our desire to accumulate and amass more things, and keeps in perspective the concrete material needs of others who lack such basic necessities. The more we consume, the less others have. The more we hoard,

15. Cavanaugh, *Being Consumed*, 35.
16. Ibid., 43.

the more we deprive others. The more we pollute, the greater the danger to creation. The less we care as we consume, the more hard-hearted we become—indifferent to the desires, justice, and care of God.

It is here that spirituality and morality are intertwined, and why our care for the earth's goods and our use of resources is a matter of Christian spirituality as well as ethics. It is true that "where your treasure is, there your heart will be also" (Matt 6:21). Our lives will be ordered by what we ultimately treasure and desire. While simplicity starts with the commitment to seek first God's kingdom, this seeking of God's kingdom produces a growing determination to live according to its values when it comes to how we spend money, and what we do with the resources that God gives us. Mother Teresa's oft-quoted adage bears repeating here: Live simply so that others may simply live. We need growth in virtues to learn to live simply so that others may simply live.

Dispositions and Actions: The Virtues of Self-Control and Gratitude

Our commitments to simplicity refocus and reclarify our priorities so that we might better discern what it is we need as opposed to what we want. In doing so, we may be able to live with limitations and within our means—and with gratitude. Self-control and gratitude are complementary virtues that shape dispositions and behavior so that our Christian formation will be of service to those with whom we share the planet, and become a means by which God's desire for justice is realized.

It is with trepidation that I raise the issue of self-control. In elementary school, I frequently received "unsatisfactory" in self-control. I never was quite sure what this meant, though it inevitably led to getting grounded by my parents. Self-control has also received a bad rap in much of Christian tradition for an unhealthy approach to our bodies that results in perverse forms of self-denial and abuse. Questions about self-control also ought to be examined when it is translated to an obsession with our bodies and appearances, especially for women, or when women's bodies become the site of control by others.[17] Self-control does not stem from a hatred of our

---

17. See the fascinating work by Griffith, *Born Again Bodies*. Her study of diet programs points to the sad irony of our obsession with bodies. Diet programs are incredibly expensive and capitalize on the already conflicted views that women tend to have about their bodies. So while the diet programs Griffith explores purport self-control, there is almost no regard for starving people around the world in these programs.

bodies that must be reined in, controlled, and denied. Its proper end is not health *per se*, though this may be one of its results; nor it is a beautification program of weight loss. Self-control is a virtue, a good, a fruit of the Spirit that is important for others as well as for us.

What is self-control? Harkening back to our reflections on Galatians 5, self-control is listed as a fruit of the Spirit (Gal 5:23). It is the capacity to direct and shape our desires, to restrain and retrain them, not deny them. In moral thought, self-control is akin to temperance, one of the four cardinal virtues along with justice, fortitude, and prudence. Temperance is the virtue that most specifically deals with how we order and manage our desires. It does not assume that desires are bad, but that they can become disordered and misdirected, resulting in damage to ourselves and others. The virtue of temperance "tempers" our inordinate and excessive desires by helping us direct them to their proper end, which is honoring God and loving others. We need not be at the whim of our desires; as persons created in God's image with various degrees of moral agency and power, we have a say in what desires we will pursue and how we should order them. As a virtue, self-control helps us avoid the excesses and extremes of unbridled consumption and rigid self-denial of basic needs. It enables us to put into perspective how God's desires might moderate and guide our own desires to consume.

As creatures, God has gifted us with desires that enrich our lives and enable us to pursue tangible and intangible needs for survival, such things as relationships, beauty, food, shelter, healthy ecosystems, clothing, and work. Yet, as happens with all good gifts from God, sin's distorting effects pushes these desires out of the bounds of God's desires and to extremes. The ends they serve are no longer God's but instead our own fulfillment, our whimsical and passing fancies, and our insatiable hunger for more. Our need for sustainable employment and wages becomes distorted by the inordinate amount of energy and time we give to work simply to get ahead or get more. Relationships, meant to give and sustain life, become all-consuming, closing in on themselves, ceasing to be places of mutual self-giving and love as we demand that all of our needs and desires be met by others. Our desire for beauty becomes a perverted obsession with appearances, while our need for clothing turns into twenty-four-hour shopping sprees. Our need for shelter becomes the desire for ever bigger spaces to house fewer people.

Self-control is a necessary means by which our desires might be reordered to better ends that are related to God's concern for all persons.

It is a crucial virtue and practice for modifying and moderating our consumption practices. Others and our creation *need* us to control and redirect our consumption practices. Samuel Powell reminds us that moderation in consumption is first of all "a faithful response to the gospel, a response that happens to have a positive if small effect on environmental problems."[18] This requires us to think more deeply about our consumption practices since, as Powell also affirms, "moderation characterizes Christians as the sort of people who are mindful of their relation to material goods."[19] We need to be more moderate in how and what we consume. We also need to stop certain practices in our buying and selling as a form of resistance to the all-pervasive nature of our market society that so shapes our desires and what we think we need to live meaningful lives.

As we learn to relate differently to material goods, and to see the good gifts of God in creation, we develop a complementary virtue to self-control, namely, gratitude.[20] While self-control tempers our misdirected desires, gratitude is a practice that offers thanks for what we already have. Gratitude is a practiced response to God's abundance and the various gifts we have been given. A primary place where we express our gratitude to God, according to Stephen Long, is the Eucharist, our remembering of the gifts that God has offered us in Christ.[21] We stand ready to receive God's gift of life with others who also receive this gift. This most solemn and worshipful participation in the Eucharist has deeply social dimensions that extend beyond our gratitude to God in recognition of our gratitude for others in a constant exchanging of gifts in our everyday lives. In other words, we give and receive "eucharistically" each day as grateful people. Long writes, "The gift that is the Eucharist is the gift that obligates its consumers to love one's neighbor as Christ loved us all. Just as Christ refused disobedience even to the point of the cross, so should we; as Christ shared food with others, so should we; as Christ dispossessed himself, so should we. Those believers who dine on the body of Christ become Christ's body as they pledge to imitate his love."[22]

---

18. Powell, *Theology of Christian Spirituality*, 190.

19. Ibid., 190.

20. See the recent book by Pohl, *Living into Community*. She provides a rich exploration of practices of gratitude.

21. Long and York, "Remembering: Offering Our Gifts," 332–45.

22. Ibid., 342.

This fundamental participation in God's divine life "reorders our everyday exchanges" and refashions our relationships; we reject scarcity and competition as primary values in our dealings with others.[23] Gratitude to God prompts a thankful giving *and* receiving of gifts that are offered us in all sorts of ways. Part of gratitude is recognition that the abundance we have has so little to do with whether or not we are worthy or entitled to such abundance, just like the gift of God's own life for our own.

A few years ago, I was in a workshop at a local social services agency that is doing important work in my community. Their resources and facilities are generously shared, and without their presence, the poor would become even more invisible and at risk. As discussions centered on extending welcome to all in the name of Christ, certain tensions began to emerge pertaining to whether or not helping the poor was a form of enablement. Behind all of this were assumptions that the poor are poor because they are lazy or made bad choices, resulting in certain predicaments. In other words, there are the poor who deserve to be poor and the poor who are truly deserving of our help. What riles me is how little we wonder about the deserving rich. Why are we reluctant to ask whether or not those who are wealthy deserve to be wealthy? Do we just assume that wealth is the reward for hard work? Does the CEO making at a very minimum ten times more than the hourly wage earner working double shifts really work harder, and is she therefore more deserving of wealth? Practices of gratitude reminds us that privileges and benefits afforded to us are not always things we have earned but instead have been given to us because of our class location, racial privilege, or access to social capital. This should be sobering for us, tempering our quickness to see our abundance as entitlement and a reward for our sense of self-righteousness.

Gratitude is being thankful for what we have, acknowledging that what we have received is, for the most part, due to the work and labor of others. While affirming that the earth is the Lord's and all that it is in it, we live in a world where goods and services at our disposal are provided by others. We should be grateful to God *and* to others for their work in providing what we need. It is this reality that Martin Luther King realized during his preaching and civil rights activism in the 1960s. "All men [*sic*] are interdependent. . . . We are everlasting debtors to unknown men and women. When we arise in the morning, we go into the bathroom where we reach for a sponge which is provided for us by a Pacific Islander. We reach for soap that is created for

23. Ibid., 343.

us by a European. Then at the table we drink coffee which is provided for us by a South American, or tea by a Chinese or cocoa by a West African. Before we leave for our jobs we are already beholden to more than half of the world."[24]

We should be grateful for what we have and express this to the myriad people who provide services to us. I am often embarrassed in restaurants when friends ignore the waitstaff and treat them rudely. Or when we, in our impatience and arrogance, call the person on the other end of the phone attempting to help us an "idiot." One of our local grocery stores employs workers of all sorts of abilities and offers training and employment that sometimes slows the line down a bit. Instead of harrumphing, might we be grateful for such employers and opportunities for belonging and wage earning? Expressing gratitude, saying thanks, and showing appreciation are central to Christian faith and practice. We are grateful to God, and grateful for others. Since our lives are bound up with the good of others, we ought to abundantly express gratitude in a variety of ways. One way of expressing gratitude might be choosing to live more intentionally and modestly in what we consume for the sake of God and God's loved creation. Perhaps practicing gratitude helps us crave simplicity, while simplicity helps us become more grateful for how little we actually need to enjoy life with God and with others.

Embodied Spirituality and Morality: Possibilities for Practices

As we think about exploring simplicity as a way of life, the need for learning and practicing the virtues of self-control and gratitude, and the impact on how we relate to and use resources, Sharon Daloz Parks articulates well the tensions and conundrums this may present for us. She writes:

> The practice of simplicity is an orientation to life that can, over time, foster a sense of right proportion and right relation within the dynamic and interdependent household of the whole earth community. *Practicing simplicity is not, however, simple. . . .* Mere streamlining, budget cutting, reengineering, throwing out, living without sacrificing, and returning to earlier, more "simple" patterns—all in the name of "simplicity"—can be useless, counterproductive, even cruel behavior. It is difficult to simplify life by leaving a demanding job if the move means losing access to group

24. King, *Where Do We Go from Here?*, 181.

health insurance. It may be complicated to change the purchasing practice of your company when low cost and low environment impact must both be taken into account. To choose simplicity as a practice is to live into complicated questions without easy answers, taking one step at a time, one step that may make another step possible.[25]

Out of the three practices explored in this book, becoming different kinds of consumers and adjusting our consumption practices may be the most difficult. Our lives are so intertwined with buying and selling—made much more complicated by the global nature of our economy—that it's overwhelming to know where to start. But start somewhere we must if we want our desires and practices to undergo a significant conversion. What small steps might we take toward simplicity—in our homes, our communities, our churches, and our places of employment? What might be some embodied practices that help us learn self-control and gratitude as we desire simplicity and work toward the manifestation of God's desires for all creation?

In her book *Family Ethics: Practices for Christians,* Julie Hanlon Rubio reminds us that for the majority of us, there is an "everydayness" to our ethical choices. This "ethics of ordinary life" requires us to recognize that our moral sensibilities are formed in families and other significant communities, where we learn how to live in respectful relationships with one another.[26] She suggests five practices for families and those living in intentional community that have the power to shape our ethic, which helps us become more cognizant of how our behavior and choices affect others. The practices she explores are sexual fidelity, eating habits, tithing, serving, and prayer. All have an important part to play in facilitating our growth in self-control and gratitude in our everyday activities. Of most immediate relevance to the concerns of this chapter is Rubio's call for us to pay attention to what and how we eat, and how we give our money. She writes that "Christian families have an obligation to think about where the food they eat comes from in order to make their eating practice coherent with their beliefs in justice and solidarity."[27] This involves being aware of how our food is produced, and the distances involved from its production to a market and to our tables. In order to have fresh produce year round (meaning the

25. Parks, "Household Economics," 50. Emphasis mine.
26. Rubio, *Family Ethics*, 4.
27. Ibid., 146.

kind of fresh produce *we* want), we will pay more, with much of the cost going to transportation and packaging—and not to those who produce and harvest our food. Food made for our convenience is often well packaged to preserve it, adding more plastic and other wrappings to the environment in addition to making food more expensive. We continue to waste food in sinful proportions.

So, what's a consumer to do? We can start by first *thinking* about what we consume. We can commit to purchasing less and using more of what we already have in our pantries and cupboards. We can join a co-op that makes food more local and accessible to communities. We can participate in Community Supported Agriculture and local farmers' markets. We can reduce our portion sizes for health reasons and to save food we might normally throw out. Rubio specifically suggests that we cut down on our consumption of meat, since "current consumption levels are unsustainable" and "place high demands on land, energy and waste."[28] She goes on to note that "if families could aim to cut their weekly meat consumption from the average of three pounds per person to one pound, this would bring the industrialized world closer to the developing world's levels. This would constitute a fairer sharing of the world's resources and a more sustainable practice."[29] We can make simpler meals by using cookbooks such as *More-with-Less* and *Extending the Table*, which raise our awareness of how people around the world make their meals, the ingredients available to them, and the portions they provide for families.[30] We can try our hand at raising a vegetable garden and giving away what it abundantly produces to others or agencies that help with food distribution (think of all the zucchini and peppers you have received from the gardening work of others!).

Another important ordinary practice germane to the concerns of this chapter is the practice of giving. The Bible is not silent on the dangers that money, wealth, and hoarding present to our souls and the needs of others. I remain surprised by the number of Christians who profess a commitment to the authority of the Bible but who are unaware of or indifferent to the emphasis in Scripture on how we should view money and property. Might we need to recover the practice of reading Scripture with an attention to the imbalances in wealth and property? Do we need to read Scripture again

---

28. Ibid., 147.

29. Ibid., 147–48.

30. Both cookbooks are projects of the Mennonite Central Committee and published by Herald Press.

and again with an eye to God's concern for the poor? One powerful source to draw our attention to what Scripture has to say about what we own and how we consume is *The Economics of Honor: Biblical Reflections on Money and Property*.[31] In rereading Scripture, we might see—some of us for the first time, others in fresh ways—how tithing and other forms of generosity bring spirituality and morality together. As Rubio summarizes:

> In the Hebrew Bible, tithing comes from the gratitude due God for all the gifts of life and the duty of those with more than enough to care for their less fortunate neighbors. The New Testament offers a combination of challenging hard sayings about wealth that distracts followers from the path of discipleship, the witness of Jesus' radically simple lifestyle, and acknowledgement . . . that wealth, provision for one's family, and even nonnecessary spending are not evil in themselves. Similarly, the early church fathers gave believers much to worry about in their reminders that superfluous spending not given to the poor results in the death of innocents and the growing moral indifference of those who fail to give. . . . With gratitude, concern for the poor, and acknowledgement of the dangers of wealth, Christians must seek a practice that enables them to delight in abundance, give away enough to keep themselves on the right path, and aid those who cannot provide for themselves.[32]

We must be intentional and thoughtful in our giving. Practices of giving resources are crucial to the well-being of others and reorient our desires and affections away from things to the desires of God for justice and mercy. In my own Wesleyan tradition, practices of giving are grounded in our belief that God's good creation must be sustained and cared for, that wealth can be dangerous, and that we have a responsibility to the poor. Our attitudes and use of money are matters for Christian spirituality and morality. Wesley was not shy in talking about money and the threat that riches presented to our spiritual and moral sensibilities. Wesley is known for his clear teaching on how we are to "gain all we can" as we earn income in just ways, attentive to the harm of our business practices on others. We are to "save all we can" by frugal and moderate means of living so that we do not hoard or waste resources. We are to "give all we can," using only that which we need so that we might give generously to meet the needs of others.

31. Haan, *Economics of Honor*.

32. Rubio, *Family Ethics*, 177.

Foster also offers concrete suggestions for how we might learn to live with less while expressing gratitude and generosity. He is realistic that there will be no perfect solutions given how enmeshed our lives are with economic practices. Yet we can make important starts and take necessary steps.[33] We need to become aware of how advertisements foster insecurity and dissatisfaction with what we already have, and we must resist their allure by trusting in God and good, honest relationships with others. We need to bring our consumption practices into the light of day as a matter of Christian discipleship. Planning for how we spend and on what is important to avoid the compulsive and unnecessary buying of items we don't need. By giving gifts that are meaningful and less trinket-like, we cut down on the stuff in our homes. For example, we have treated nieces to a local university play, giving them a weekend at the "Reuschling B and B" as gifts. We purchase jams and food items from local farmers for presents. The possibilities for alternative gift exchanges are myriad and well worth pursuing.

While there are many suggestions for better practices in how we spend money and consume resources, it's important to remember that practices are also forms of resistance to prevailing norms. Perhaps it's a tougher task to see how we might resist consumerism by refusing to participate in particular practices. Perhaps a Sabbath from consumption is important for learning self-control, practicing gratitude, and focusing on others.[34] According to Wirzba, practicing Sabbath is a matter of life and death—and a matter of justice for God's entire creation. Practicing Sabbath is a form of freedom that appreciates the power to say no to urgency and to the routines that so engross our days. Designating a day when we won't shop and refraining from buying new clothes we don't need are ways of resisting the pull to consume. Picking a practice to resist the all-encompassing nature of our consumer society can be an important way to retrieve God's sense of holiness and justice in creation by taking a break, being grateful to God, and saying no to what would otherwise consume us and shape our desires so that we might say yes to God and God's desires for justice.[35]

33. I am summarizing suggestions from chapters 7–10 in *Freedom of Simplicity.*

34. See Owens, "Sabbath-Keeping," and Wirzba, *Living the Sabbath.*

35. See the rich work by Dawn, *The Sense of the Call,* especially chapter 4, "Freedom to Say No—And, Therefore, Yes."

Conclusion

"Living simply so that others may simply live" is great for bumper stickers. It is greater still when practiced in concrete ways that teach us self-control and gratitude as consumers. Consuming is inevitable; extricating ourselves from the complexities and complicities of our global economy is nearly impossible. But we can be more morally responsible participants by becoming aware of how our lives are related to others, and how the goods we consume affect the good of others. Simply starting to consume differently, more wisely and justly, is a first step to living simply, with gratitude for God's good gifts and graces. This God desires as we are shaped more and more to desire justice and express this in simplicity and self-control.

six

Confession and Resistance

ANYONE WHO HAS EXPERIENCED a split between factions in his or her church knows how damaging it can be. I experienced one soon after graduating from seminary when I joined the staff of a large, nondenominational evangelical church. The rending occurred gradually, hidden by growth that was proclaimed as success. The issues that contributed to the unresolved conflicts were numerous: "old guard" versus "new guard," introduction of new worship services and styles, differing understandings of the mission of the church, personality conflicts, and plain old power struggles. The gradual tearing apart of this congregation came to a head when the unwise actions of the senior pastor were brought to light. Even though the events occurred eight years prior to this major point of conflict, they personalized the dimensions of the split in very harmful ways. No longer were we as a church community responsible for the conflicts, dissensions, and harmful attitudes and behaviors that had been building over the years. It was one person who was responsible who needed to confess and repent. After that, he was fired.

As a relative newcomer to this church, I was unaware of the many hidden dynamics that were going on. Yet I had been around enough to observe some significant differences on how we understood confession, forgiveness, reconciliation, restoration, and mutual responsibilities for our sin. At one of many contentious meetings called to air grievances and find ways forward, one of my dear ministry colleagues called us all to confession and repentance. In response, one of the church leaders said, "Why do I have to repent? I didn't do anything wrong." Wow. Where to start?

I continue to think about this experience for the many ways it has informed my interest in the integration of spirituality and morality. It has been a reminder for me of how dangerous it is to claim a particular kind of righteousness in one's relationship with God with a disregard for righteousness and justice in our dealings with others, and to shun *even the possibility* that we have contributed to our corporate problems.[1] It is also a situation that makes me ponder the dynamics between personal sin and our sinful communities. It may be hard for some of us—given our locations in certain ecclesial traditions that have been so influenced by aspects of American individualism, as this church was—to see the corporate dimensions of sin in which we participate. This is a trend observed by Michael Emerson and Christian Smith in their important book, *Divided by Faith: Evangelical Religion and the Problem of Race in America.*[2] In their study of evangelical attitudes about race and racialization in American society, Emerson and Smith note the sociocultural tools in the "toolbox" of many white evangelicals: accountable free will individualism, relationalism, and antistructuralism.[3] These tools predispose us to interpret social-ethical issues and corporate dynamics through deeply personalized lenses. Our responses to solving problems tend to be located at an individual level; problems are often blamed on the bad behavior of a few who need to get their act together or go away. We think that we can make a difference by establishing personal relationships while blinded by the ways in which our relationships are deeply influenced and mediated by the social contexts in which they are formed. The results are degrees of befuddlement when it comes to addressing such social-ethical issues as the abuse of power, structured racism and sexism, and various other injustices in our corporate ethos and practices.

In this chapter, I will extend my reflection on the integration of spirituality and morality by exploring the practices of confession and resistance. What is confession? How does confession relate to our acknowledgment of our participation in wrongdoing? Do individuals alone confess, or is there a call for corporate confession for the wrongs *we* have done? What are the virtues needed for becoming people who are able to see our own sin, confess it, and resist participation in wrongdoing? As in previous chapters, I will frame my proposal by focusing on our desire for God and the things of God as central to Christian formation, and how these practices of confession and resistance facilitate good for others as well as for ourselves. I

---

1. I address this concern in greater detail in my book *Reviving Evangelical Ethics*, chapter 4.

2. Emerson and Smith, *Divided by Faith.*

3. Ibid., 76.

will explore the virtues of humility and hope necessary for confession and resistance, and what these practices might look like in our all-too-real communities with their potentialities and pitfalls.

Practices of Confession and Resistance

What is confession? Etymologically, "confession" means to "acknowledge or agree with" someone or something. Confession is the act of speaking about what is known, true, and real. In Christian thought, confession has two dimensions. First is our confession, our acknowledgment of God as God and Christ as Lord (Rom 10:9–13). Confession is part of our public proclamation with other Christians throughout history and around the globe of what we believe is true about the Triune God at the heart of Scripture's story and articulated in creeds we confess in our corporate gatherings. From the Nicene Creed we confess, "We believe in One God . . . We believe in One Lord, Jesus Christ . . . We believe in the Holy Spirit." This kind of confession is a fundamental aspect of our Christian witness that, according to Nicholas Adams, extends beyond the mere words we recite to the kinds of lives we commit to live.[4] When we confess the creeds, we do a kind of reasoning wherein we make connections between the various parts and how they relate to the whole, recognizing the importance of these connections for bringing our speaking and actions together. We engage in a form of witness and commitment-making when we make confessions about the Triune God. Adams writes:

> To say the Creed is to face up to gifts and responsibilities. This does not mean that Christians need to overcome all obstacles and injustices before they may utter it: absolutism of this kind encourages procrastination and ultimately leads to despair. Rather it means that saying the Creed means making a promise: a promise to "believe in," to commit to, God's description of the world and no other. What remains after this is hard work, and a readiness to receive the gifts that make it possible. . . . To say the Creed is for a community to proclaim itself engaged in it. And, because it is uttered publicly, it is to invite the rest of the world to hold us to that promise, and join us in our work.[5]

4. Adams, "Confessing the Faith," 207–21.
5. Ibid., 219–20.

Confession goes beyond merely saying something with our words. This is always the danger of reciting words by rote without thinking about what one is *actually* saying and confessing. There are challenges at both spectrums of Christian tradition. In more formalized liturgical traditions, there is always the danger of saying what we do not mean because we aren't thinking about what we are confessing. There is an equal danger, however, that we won't confess what we should about what we believe and about our human condition in traditions that eschew the gifts of the creeds and confessions as meaningless repetitions. We must say what we mean, and mean what we say, in order to have a modicum of integrity in our central confessions of Christian faith and practice. Our speech and actions matter when it comes to confessing our central claims about who God is and what this means for our lives.

The Scriptures remind us that a confession of what we believe is not only with our lips but also with our lives. We acknowledge that God is the loving sovereign Lord not just by what we say but by what we do. This is a primary concern addressed in the epistles of John. While we "test the spirits" to discern the Spirit of Christ, we do so with a confession that "Jesus Christ has come in the flesh" and "is from God" (1 John 4:3). Yet this confession is also confirmed by the kind of love that Christians have for one another. Our confession of Christ as Lord, while theologically accurate, is hollow and ineffective without loving as Jesus loves. John offers these chilling words: "Those who say, 'I love God,' and hate their brothers or sisters, are liars; for those who do not love a brother or sister whom they have seen, cannot love God whom they have not seen. The command we have from him is this: those who love God must love their brothers and sisters also" (1 John 4:20–21).

Confession also has another dimension in Christian thought and practice in that we confess our sins before God and with others. Confession is "to acknowledge or agree with" God and others about the wrongs we have done by bringing them to light. When we confess our sin, we acknowledge what God already knows about us, and what others likely know about us as well. For this reason, I remain unconvinced that there are such things as "hidden sins," while there are many unspoken and unacknowledged ones, and sins of which we are unaware. Our sin affects others whether it's acknowledged or not. Again, we find unnerving words in 1 John for our unwillingness to acknowledge our sin: "If we say we have no sin, we deceive ourselves, and the truth is not in us. . . . If we say that we have not sinned, we make him a liar, and his word is not in us" (1 John 1:8, 10). However, here is our hope: "If we confess our sins, he who is faithful and just, will forgive us our sins and cleanse us from all unrighteousness" (1 John 1:9).

Confession is offered in the context of a relationship with the God who knows and loves us still, and has desires for our lives that we cannot even begin to imagine. Confession of our sin signals our profound understanding of our need for forgiveness, fresh starts, and newness of life. While a sobering and humbling experience, confession is also a hopeful one. With confession and repentance, there is hope and there is freedom in forgiveness that the sins that haunt us need not control us when they are brought to light as we ask God and our sisters and brothers in Christ for help.

There is a wonderful irony in confession. While our bookstores are filled with self-help resources, and as spirituality has been co-opted by the expressive individualism of "finding our true selves" in order to feel better about ourselves, practices of confession require and facilitate the kind of self-understanding and awareness that we so desperately seek and that is so necessary for change.[6] Confession itself is an important act of self-discovery and a means by which we speak the truth about ourselves to God and others, always in the context of God's love, grace, and the gift of the Holy Spirit for better ways of being the kinds of persons God desires us to be. David deSilva suggests that when practiced regularly, confession "helps us arrive at a more genuine knowledge of ourselves."[7] Its effects are profound:

> Self-examination and confession is not just a mental exercise. We sin with our whole being; we need to repent with our whole being. We need to allow ourselves to feel genuine sorrow, engaging our hearts as well as our minds in this discipline. This does not mean subjecting ourselves to feelings of inadequacy or guilt, as if piety meant self-loathing. Rather, it is an exercise in appreciating the full import of our sinful choices, attitudes and lifestyles, so that we can comprehend the depth of God's mercy and compassion toward us and, experiencing a fuller measure of gratitude toward him, be catapulted into greater degrees of love toward God and our neighbor.[8]

6. See the important work by Bellah et al., *Habits of the Heart*. While their work studies primarily white Protestant religious expressions, their insights for the ways in which religious practices and conceptions of spirituality have become avenues for "expressive individualism" and self-discovery are important. See also Roof, *Spiritual Marketplace*.

7. deSilva, *Sacramental Life*, 101.

8. Ibid., 104–5.

To know ourselves is to be known by God and to grasp what it is that God knows about us. We are loved by God, capable of imaging God in profound ways, and prone to wandering from the God we profess to love. We confess and acknowledge a variety of realities: our deep beliefs in the Triune God; our profound gratitude for God's love and grace; the myriad ways in which we fail to live out what we believe, with detrimental effects on our neighbor; our lack of understanding about ourselves; and our need for God's forgiveness and grace that offer us always new ways forward. When we confess in faith, "we turn from self-absorption, self-preoccupation, pride, and self-reliance" in order to receive forgiveness and the freedom that comes with it to "turn from sin and to live in the light."[9]

Confession as acknowledgment of our sin is also a practice of resistance that sin need not master us. In Romans, Paul seems to indicate that we are set free by Christ in order to become slaves of righteousness and not remain as slaves of sin (Rom 6:21–23). This is interesting because it is not a denial of human sin. Paul boldly acknowledges the power of sin that seeks to dominate our mortal bodies, our entire being, and control our "passions" (*epithumia*, also translated as "desires"). For Paul, sin perverts our passions so that we live as if disordered desires must always hold sway over us and are somehow ultimate in what they say about our human condition. We will obey that which we think has power in our lives. For Paul, however, there is another Master and another word about our human condition now that we have been "set free from sin, having become slaves of righteousness" (Rom 6:18). As elsewhere in the New Testament, righteousness is *dikaiosunē*, also translated as "justice," bringing together the sense that righteousness in Christ propels us to live with justice in right relationships with God and others that require rightly ordered desires.

Confession of our sin becomes a form of resistance in that as we acknowledge what enslaves us, and so disorders our desires, we need not let this be the final word about our lives. Stating what is true in confession about our misdirected passions, and our slavery to and complicities in injustice, is also an act of commitment. We confess in order to be and do differently. We acknowledge our lack of desire for righteousness and justice, because the pursuit of our own disordered desires becomes more important. We confess the kinds of lives we have been set free to live. We are made righteous in Christ in order to live according to justice and righteousness. This choice is evident in Paul's words to the Roman Christians: "so now

9. Smith, "Penitence," 663.

present your members as slaves to righteousness for sanctification" (Rom 6:19). Confession is a bold acknowledgment of Christ's power to rescue us from sin, and of Christ's lordship to shape our ultimate desires and passions for the kind of righteousness and justice for which we have been set free, and which God desires for human life.

Our confession of Christ as Lord is also a necessary practice of resistance that makes clear and public our ultimate loyalties against ideologies, idols, and ever present co-opting and politicizing agents of Christian faith.[10] Confession is a statement of our ultimate loves and a way of being held accountable to live according to what we profess is ultimately good, desirous, noble, true, and just. As such, confession becomes a means by which we resist the evils and harms that come with leaving areas of our lives outside the purview of God's grace, mercy, and justice. If Christ is Lord, then all areas of life—the public and the personal, the social and the individual, the sacred and the profane—must be open to and under the purview of the love, justice, and mercy of God. Resistance calls us to say yes to Christ as Lord and no to those things that deny the goodness of God and wreak havoc in human lives and communities.

Our communities and institutions can have a totalizing impact on our lives in ways that skew our priorities and subordinate our moral commitments. Resistance as a practice is needed when groups, institutions, and other social bodies submerge alternative voices that attempt to say no to the status quo. Saying "no" to a particular set of arrangements that subvert God's desires for justice and mercy also involves speaking a "yes" to other possibilities of relating to each other in our common life. This is an important contribution that various liberation theologians make to an "ethic of resistance."[11] Rosita deAnn Mathews explores a variety of practices of resistance in systems where "certain acceptable behaviors, which are normative within a corporate setting, may challenge a personal ethic of work and relationship."[12] The prime example of resistance, according to Mathews, is Jesus. What comes to mind are the temptation narratives in the wilderness where the devil presented promises to Jesus, which ironically the devil

10. See Míguez Bonino, *Toward a Christian Politic Ethics*, for an important distinction between a politicization of Christianity and a Christian ethics of politics, particularly chapter 1, "The Need for a Political Ethics."

11. See the following works: Bedford, "Little Moves against Destructiveness"; Míguez Bonino, *Toward a Christian Politic Ethics*; Crysdale, *Embracing Travail*, chapter 3; Welch, *Feminist Ethic of Risk*; and the series of essays in Townes, *Troubling in My Soul*.

12. Mathews, "Using Power from the Periphery," 93.

had no right to promise (Matt 4:1–13; Mark 1:12–13; Luke 4:1–13). The devil appealed to Jesus to use acceptable and self-serving forms of power to get what Jesus deserved: food, power, honor, recognition, and reward for obedience and allegiance. Yet Jesus resisted and provided an alternative by naming the false promises that the devil made, trusting in God, and rejecting the temptation to follow ways that were contrary to God's redemptive purposes. These actions put Jesus at risk, illuminating that resistance and the use of power in alternative ways carry with them certain peril. Crysdale notes the impact of Jesus' ethic of risk:

> In accepting death as the expected consequence of claiming his (w)holy identity, Jesus revealed the character of God as well as the nature of human identity. God, it turns out, is not like the Powers, is not a wrathful God demanding justice at all costs. God refused to battle with the Powers on their own terms. He would not use violence to promote his cause. Instead, in allowing Jesus' death, and in raising him from the dead, God revealed that there is permanence and transcendence to human identity that evil cannot destroy. Authentic resistance is the claiming of that identity and a refusal to damage it through capitulating to power tactics. Authentic resistance thus becomes a statement of faith in eternal life, meaning confidence that one's identity perdures in God's embrace in spite of the oppressive definition of others.[13]

This is, as Mathews notes, a form of "power from the periphery" which "resists evil by utilizing alternative action. The response is not one of passivity but of denying the aggressor the opportunity to define our method of resistance."[14] This kind of resistance requires strength, a clear sense of what it is that God desires for human life, and seeing how the systems and institutions that we inhabit subvert these desires. Mathews wants to remind us that we are agents in these systems and have various means of resisting injustice. We do so by saying no to acceptable ways of using power and others as means to dubious ends. We also say yes to using power modeled

---

13. Crysdale, *Embracing Travail*, 55. It is important to note that Crysdale is not advocating a redemptive theology that justifies the sacrifice of victims for a greater good. She recognizes the ways in which penal substitution models of the atonement may expect and justify a kind of suffering that is detrimental to those suffering. In her ethic of risk, exercising an alternative mode of power is itself an act of power and agency that redefines the meaning of one's actions.

14. Mathews, "Using Power from the Periphery," 93.

on Jesus' own strength of identity and commitment to God's ways of justice and righteousness.

Desire for God and the Things of God

Personal confession is important and, when made seriously, can become a significant means for resistance to that which enslaves our passions and desires. Public confession can be powerful for bringing our various voices together in a resounding yes to God's desires for justice, mercy, and humility, and a resounding no to the injustice, violence, and arrogance that destroy human life. We confess our belief in God and reaffirm our allegiance to God's kingdom in order to resist all other gods or idols that would draw us away from our ultimate desires for relationship with God and a life ordered by the justice that God loves and desires for creation. We are reminded in Scripture that "the Lord loves justice" (Ps 11:7) and desires justice, mercy, and humility (Mic 6:8). Our confession becomes a means of embodying God's desires for our lives, especially for humility and righteousness in all of our ways.

Confession is an avenue for speaking into existence the kind of justice and righteousness that should be the passions that reign in our "mortal bodies" and the passions we have been set free by Christ to pursue and live out. As deSilva notes, confession is not just a cathartic exercise in self-pity or self-loathing. Instead, it is "an exercise in appreciating the full import of our sinful choices, attitudes and lifestyles, *so that* we can comprehend the depth of God's mercy and compassion toward us and, experiencing a fuller measure of gratitude toward him, be catapulted into greater degrees of love toward God and our neighbor."[15] Confession acknowledges our failures to desire God and to order our lives around what God desires. We confess our sins of commission, the things we have done that have defied God and God's purpose for human life. Yet also we acknowledge our sins of omission, those behaviors, attitudes, and perspectives that have kept us from doing what we ought to have done. In my own life, the motivation in sins of omission is less ignorance than it is apathy. I need to confess that I often do not care, am too busy, or I shun the inconvenience in making the necessary adjustments to my prized priorities and use of time in order to attend to the concerns that concern God. I am sadly much more willing to leave things

15. deSilva, *Sacramental Life*, 104–5. Italics mine.

as they are in order to suit my needs and satisfy my desires for comfort, convenience, and control.

Confession is a practice of truth telling. Confession acknowledges the realities about ourselves and also about how things really are in our churches and institutions and in the world. As such, it becomes an act of bringing to light what has been hidden and skewed in our common life in order to "live in the light" of God's goodness and desires for justice in our relationships. Truth telling is an aspect of naming and identifying our failures for the purpose of owning and correcting them. We can do something about our wrongdoing and injustice. In order to do this, according to Miroslav Volf, we must "remember rightly" in order to confess truthfully.[16] For Volf, telling the truth rightly is a moral obligation. Even with our spotty and selective memories, we are still responsible for telling the truth truthfully, neither minimizing wrongdoing nor exaggerating wrongs done. Volf writes that "our moral obligation to tell the truth is heightened if a story reflects *well or badly* on our own character or that of another person."[17] We all want to look better than we actually are, and we want our actions to appear less tainted and nobler than they were really were. Conversely, we want others to look worse than they actually might have been. If the truth is not told in such a way that we clearly name the wrongs done, then we remain as we were, whether victims or perpetrators in injustice (or both, as the case may be). The circumstances remain as they were, now woven into the fabric of wrongdoing that affects all of us, with little movement forward to God's desires for the reshaping of our lives.

While telling the truth rightly is a form of justice, so is failing to confess or to remember rightly an act of injustice. Remembering wrongly by victims and perpetrators propagates and reinforces the web of injustices through denial, minimization, or exaggeration. What's interesting about Volf's insights is the ways in which victims may exacerbate injustice by failing to remember rightly the wrongs done to them. This is not a "blame the victim" game for wrongs done but instead a necessary aspect of reconciliation. It is easy to blame victims and just as easy to blame perpetrators of wrong. When exaggeration coincides with a wrongdoer's denials and refusals to confess, the pathway to reconciliation and true justice becomes almost impossible to find. Injustices are exacerbated and the road to reconciliation

16. Volf, *End of Memory.* See also the recent work by my colleague Craig Hovey, *Bearing True Witness.*

17. Volf, *End of Memory*, 54. Italics in original.

and restoration becomes much bumpier and longer when truth telling is skirted for easy answers and quick solutions to problems. We may run from acknowledging our complicities in wrongdoing but ultimately can never hide them.

In order for confession to be truthful, just, and restorative, the wrongs we do must be remembered accurately and not fabricated or exaggerated. For this, we need practices of resistance to the ever present temptation to gloss over issues, to tell a partial story, to minimize problems, to blow them out of proportion, or to control the retelling of them so that they are more palatable. It is part of our human nature, with our fallible memories, to remember incidents in which we appear better than we actually were or in which others appear viler than they really were. We are masters at shifting blame and justifying behavior because facing the truth about ourselves is a difficult task. We will resist in all the wrong ways by perpetuating lies and faulty memories. Volf notes that in Scripture, we are commanded to refrain from bearing false witness by telling untruths about our neighbors. This is made more tragically ironic when we continue to avoid the truths about ourselves while perpetuating falsehoods about our neighbor. True confession and confession of what is true becomes a form of love and grace because it seeks to heal, help, repair, and restore. It is also a practice of resistance to defining another always as an enemy and beyond redemptive power. Confession and telling the truth about ourselves seek a justice that God desires, one that restores, not one that seeks vengeance to bolster our own sense of righteousness. Confession and truth telling are ultimately hopeful. Volf writes: "Instead, the highest aim of lovingly truthful memory seeks to bring about repentance, forgiveness, and transformation of wrong-doers, and reconciliation between wrongdoers and their victims. When these goals are achieved, memory can let go of offenses without ceasing to be truthful. For then remembering truthfully will have reached its ultimate goal in the unhindered love of neighbor."[18]

Truthful confession that acknowledges the wrongs we have done is an act of neighbor love. God desires righteousness and justice in our relationships. One way to bring this about is to acknowledge where we have failed to do justice and love mercy *so that* we can be free to start again in desiring God and the things that God desires. Confession can bring about the goods that God desires and, in doing so, embody these goods in our lives and communities.

18. Ibid., 65.

Focus on the Good of Others

Confession is not just good for the soul. It is good for all aspects of our lives. Confession produces various goods essential for just communities: honesty, openness to correction, bringing to light our secret wrangling for power, and the hope needed for always better ways of being and living together. The Truth and Reconciliation Commission in South Africa was formed to tell the truth about the past, to resist further evils, and to find pathways forward to better ways of living according to God's justice and righteousness in relationships. It is a profound example of how confession and resistance serve justice, restoration, and in so doing, help us learn to live together. After the dismantling of the brutal and genocidal apartheid regime in South Africa, and the election of Nelson Mandela as president, the Truth and Reconciliation Commission was founded and written into the constitution in order to deal with the past evils of personal and systemic violence. One of its leaders, Archbishop Desmond Tutu, working based on Christian conviction, deemed this kind of practice necessary if there was ever to be a future that was not marked by violence. His famous line is the title of his autobiography: *No Future Without Forgiveness.*[19] The practices of confession and truth telling became means of realizing justice for both victims and perpetrators. Hearing the stories of victims in all of their wrenching detail became an avenue for justice as they were heard for the first time as humans whose fundamental dignity had been violated through violence. Perpetrators had to tell their stories of violence in order to be eligible to receive amnesty for what they had done. These dual confessions by victims and perpetrators bound them together and became a means of resistance to further evil by valuing restoring justice over revenge. Archbishop Tutu acknowledges how difficult the process was, and how numerous were the skeptics and the ones who refused to participate. Yet this practice of confession produced a form of resistance that refused to let a future become defined by its evil past, at the same time honoring the moral obligation to tell the truth about the past in order to have an alternative future. Truthful confession served a common good.

Confession is good for us and for others. Christian psychologists in a recent study explored how responses of repentance, offense rumination, self-justification, and distraction affect offenders, victims, and

19. Tutu, *No Future Without Forgiveness.*

relationships.[20] Their discoveries are insightful for illuminating the "goods" carried within practices of repentance (which involves confession), and the danger of thwarting these goods when we justify our behaviors, obsess on them or deflect them, and blame others. The authors of the study note the differences between offense rumination and confession. Offense rumination reinforces a self-loathing and self-obsession that is paralyzing and incapacitating. Offense rumination is narrow and self-focused, which prevents an outward movement toward repentance, confession, and relational reconciliation. While offense rumination draws us inward in paralyzing ways, self-justification externalizes blame and continues to remove us from the relational dimensions of our offenses. In the place of rumination and rationalization are the treasured practices of confession and repentance, which can bring about the goods of restoration, healthy self-concepts, and relational repairs. They write, "In between the myopic vision of self-justification that evades responsibility and the myopic vision of offense rumination that wallows only in the negative, repentance seeks to honestly see and name one's own culpability, apologize, make amends, and cultivate new behaviors that create relational possibilities for the future."[21]

The goods of confession for ourselves and others include a greater healthy awareness of ourselves, of God's grace and power for new beginnings, and of new possibilities in our relationships with others. It is significant that psychologists trained to study the inner dimensions and external manifestations of our complex humanity affirm a practice such as confession for its spiritually and morally forming potential. They observe the ways in which confession and true repentance facilitate what is good for us: an honest telling the truth of our condition and relational ruptures with God and others *so that* they may be repaired and find new life. This is affirmed by theologians and pastoral practitioners, who see confession as a means for focusing on the good of others as well as ourselves. Everist writes, "Each of us is racist, sexist, classist and more because we participate in the human condition of inequitable power systems. Rather than debate or defend, human beings do well to confess. Because I write as a Christian I use the word 'confession' because only through confession of systemic as well as personal sin are we free to examine root causes and claim new life in Christ in order to be empowered for transformative change."[22]

20. Witvliet, Hinman, Brandt, and Exline, "Responding to Our Own Transgressions."
21. Ibid., 233.
22. Everist, "Gender, Power and Leadership," 46.

We do well to confess wrongdoing and resist evil. Confession contains a set of goods, as it is also a practice that points us forward to an alternative future marked by justice, righteousness, and peace. In order to be and become people who stand ready to confess, and who have the strength and courage to resist, we need virtues that accompany and are carried forward in these practices.

Dispositions and Actions: The Virtues of Humility and Hope

What virtues might be required for desiring to confess sin and our ultimate loyalties to Christ's lordship and his ways? What virtues might help us in our resistance to evil and in our proclivities to skip over spiritually and morally formative practices in our desire for quick solutions to complex problems such as injustice? I suggest that humility and hope are two virtues necessary for confession and resistance.

At first glance it may seem odd to suggest humility as a necessary virtue for such bold acts as confession and resistance. The kind of humility I have in mind is not the self-abasing kind that is often sadly caricatured as an anathema in a world of power and privilege. Humility is what is required and learned through ongoing and honest self-reflection as we open our lives to God and to others for better ways of understanding who we should be and what we should do. It is a disposition that fosters honesty in our relationship with God that must translate into willingness for change. We need humility in order to confess if confession is to be an act of healthy self-assessment. An epistemic humility is a posture that recognizes that we "see in a mirror, dimly" and "know only in part" (1 Cor 13:12). We are finite and limited as creatures, which is as God intended. Humility is a virtue that enables us to live with our creaturely existence as a gift of God so that we might depend on God and others for wisdom, help, and understanding. The opposite of this kind of humility is epistemological pride, as well as other forms of pride. It is the wrongheaded assurance that certain persons have all the answers and all they need to know in order to be right. Humility is a practice that is open to the reality that we could be wrong and misguided in what we perceive to be real and true. Practicing humility requires openness to correction, an interest to hear and see differently, and a willingness to learn from others so that we might see more clearly.

Stassen and Gushee explore humility in the context of Jesus' teaching in the Sermon on the Mount in the beatitude, "Blessed are the humble, for they shall inherit the earth" (Matt 5:5). They note the biblical descriptions of Moses and Jesus, who are described as humble but were in no way portrayed as meek and powerless in doing the will of God. The idea behind humility is one of surrender to the will of God and a willingness to live our lives committed to the will of God.[23] We should not miss the relationship between this humble surrender to God's will for how it relates to what God desires and requires of us. Humility, therefore, is not the surrendering of our own wills but instead a realignment of them according to God's desires. A proper understanding of Christian humility must be guided by the posture and practices of Jesus, who had a clear sense of who he was and what he was called to do on behalf of humanity. Humility is a means for forming and shaping the selves that we are and the persons whom God loves, so that we are clearer in vision about who God is, who we are, and what God desires for our lives.

An accompanying virtue to humility necessary for confession and resistance is hope. Hope is that grand theological virtue, along with faith and love, that enables us to endure the imperfections and injustices of our present realities because we trust that God's work is not yet complete. The theological grounding for hope is an eschatology that understands "God has promised that the present reality is not the final one."[24] Hope is not wild-eyed optimism or utopian denial of the difficulties that confront us, that work to impede the realization of God's reign of peace, righteousness, and justice.[25] Hope mediates our tendencies to despair about how bad things can be and our delusions of easy fixes to complex issues. There is much that should cause us to despair. Yet when this despair creates numbness in our lives, the "royal consciousness" has taken over.[26] We begin to internalize the values of the dominant culture that justifies inequalities, injustices, and oppression. Brueggemann writes that the "royal consciousness militates against hope."[27] We are unable to believe that another possibility exists for an alternative community with an alternative moral vision. The task, then, of people who dare to confess another possibility based on their trust in God and in God's desires for justice, and who resist the seduction of competing desires for power and privilege, is "*to bring people to engage the*

23. Stassen and Gushee, *Kingdom Ethics*, 40.

24. Roberts, "Eschatology and Hope," 94.

25. See Elshtain, *Who Are We?*

26. Brueggemann, *Prophetic Imagination*.

27. Ibid., 63.

promise of newness that is at work in our history with God."[28] A confession of our belief that God is still at work in the world and that God invites us to participate should produce practices of resistance to injustices that deny God's goodness and care for all of creation. We do not give up because God does not give up. God has desires for creation that have yet to be realized and offers us the bold invitation to be agents of hope in a world of despair.

Hope also tempers our misguided desires for a utopia. Practicing hope is hard. The temptation to circumvent the trust and faith that undergird our hope is ever present as we jettison the work of becoming a more hopeful people in favor of quick and superficial solutions to complex problems. Míguez Bonino cautions against our humanely constructed utopias that circumvent the ways in which God works in moving history towards its consummation in Christ.[29] His concerns are twofold. The first problem is that we confuse eschatology with utopia. When we collapse God's work into our various historical projects, we falsely equate our human constructions with God's purposes. He observes that "God's time of consummation . . . while it assumes history, does not simply crown history's achievements but also judges and transforms it."[30] God's desired future requires the hopeful human struggle for the justice and righteousness that God desires. Settling for narrow, self-interested utopian views produces a second concern for Míguez Bonino. It is the baptizing of our very human projects that serve our particular interests as we "ignore the qualitative newness of God's consummation."[31] The result is the same. Settling for something less than what God desires does not require much of us. Contentment with our own utopian projects narrows our understanding of the fullness of God's time and of God's desire for the final day when all things will be made new. Participating with God by the power of the Spirit on behalf of Christ's kingdom requires a profound trust and lived out hope that keeps us moving ahead toward this day even as we work to realize aspects of it, albeit incompletely, in our own days.

Central to Christian spirituality and morality are humility and hope. Humility is the acknowledgement of our limitations, finitude, and creaturely dependence on God. It requires vigorous and confessing self-examination before God and others so that we can acknowledge our shortcomings in

28. Ibid., 62–63. Italics in original.

29. Míguez Bonino, *Toward a Christian Political Ethics*, 90–94.

30. Ibid., 92.

31. Ibid.

order to be changed. Hope is a core longing based on what we ultimately desire in the fulfillment of God's desires for justice and righteousness. Hope grounds our practices of resistance, enabling us to see things as they are in light of what we believe they should be. In confession, we express our commitments and the ways in which we thwart God's desires. In practices of resistance, we say no to all misguided desires that harm people and yes to God's desire for justice and righteousness. By learning and practicing humility and hope, we are formed to be people who embody God's desires for making all things new.

Embodied Spirituality and Morality: Possibilities for Practices

Practices of confession are deeply personal and occur in the context of trusting relationships. We confess to God because we trust God to forgive and we confess to others because we need to hear the words, "You are forgiven." Finding a partner or a group with whom to practice regular confession is important. I gather with three close friends once a month for long and deep catch-up conversations that lay bare our struggles and sins in this most hopeful regular gathering. We confess words of grace and forgiveness in our relationships. During the Lenten season each year at my church, we are given an opportunity to pick a practice that orients us in this most holy time in the church calendar. Many of the suggested practices are ones of resistance, such as refraining from watching television, shopping, or eating unhealthy foods. Last year, I chose to practice confession with a partner once a week but sadly failed to follow up on this commitment for very flimsy reasons. I intend to follow up on this practice during the upcoming Lenten season.

Using the Scriptures to guide our confessions is important. It is hard to read Psalm 51—yet it is important. It is a powerful guide to confession and forces us to know our transgressions. As we read slowly through this psalm, we pray that the Holy Spirit will bring to mind our transgressions so that they might be fully known and we can receive forgiveness and a clean heart. I often try a reverse reading of Scripture. For example, when reading the Beatitudes, I hear the words of Jesus as he calls blessed those who mourn, who are meek, who hunger and thirst for righteousness, who are merciful and pure in heart, who are peacemakers, who are willing to be persecuted and scorned for the sake of righteousness. Rereading these Scriptures forces me to confess that I am so often *not* these things that Jesus calls good. I am not merciful or meek, nor do I always desire righteousness, especially when it is disruptive to my comfort. I don't always mourn over the injustices that grieve God's heart, and I am much more willing to seek forms of revenge than peace. The same can be tried for the grand chapter on love in 1 Corinthians: "Love is patient; love is kind; love is not envious or boastful or arrogant or rude. It does not insist on its own way; it is not irritable or resentful; it does not rejoice in wrongdoing, but rejoices in the truth. It bears all things, believes all things, hopes all things, endures all things" (1 Cor 13:4–7).

What a model of the kind of love that God desires and that too often I fail to demonstrate. By diligently paying attention to our reading of Scripture, particularly the parts that provide such contrasts to our lives with their disordered desires, we might begin a routine practice of seeing how Scripture provides the mirror into which we look to see ourselves as God sees us—dearly loved, yet still disordered in what we love and desire. The mirror of Scripture is a powerful means that God uses to sharpen and clarify our fuzzy pictures of ourselves and of God's desires for our lives.

Richard Foster recommends using the written confessions of our churches. They provide enough of a general framework in which to locate our own very specific sins. Foster notes the advantage of using formalized confessions: "First, the formalized form of the printed confession does not allow for excuses and extenuating circumstances. We must confess that we have sinned by our own fault, our own most grievous fault. Our sins cannot be called errors in judgment, nor is there any room to blame them on upbringing or family or mean neighbors. This is a Reality Therapy of the best sort since we are so prone to blame our sins on everybody and everything instead of taking personal responsibility for them."[32]

Taking time to confess is important, and guides can be helpful ways to stimulate our minds to remember sins of commission (what have we done?) and omission (what we have failed to do?). Use the *Book of Common Prayer* or *The Spiritual Exercises* by St. Ignatius of Loyola to focus prayers of confession. They help guide us to examine and reflect on the events of our lives that we might tend to ignore or dismiss as unimportant to our spiritual and moral formation. Foster also recommends keeping a diary or journal that can aid us in reflecting on experiences and events that might help explain why we respond in the ways we do. Foster cautions us to remember that confession is not an act of self-flogging and paralyzing introspection.

32. Foster, *Celebration of Discipline*, 148.

Confession is ultimately a hopeful act, one that readies us to receive God's grace and forgiveness anew, since "confession begins in sorrow, but it ends in joy. There is celebration in the forgiveness of sin because it results in a genuinely changed life."[33]

Confession is a deeply relational practice. It is important to pay equal attention to the practices of those who receive our confessions. These relationships must be trustworthy and free from manipulation. They must be marked by wisdom and respect for the confidence placed in those who hear our stories. Those who receive our confessions must be entrusted to hear and respond, and they must be willing to say, "You are forgiven."[34] This is a relationship of power. Information is shared that frees confessors, who are taking responsibility for their sin. Yet responsibility now shifts to those who have heard, who must guard and protect what has been entrusted to them. This likely assumes that those who are willing to hear us are also practicing confession with others and know firsthand the risk and responsibility this entails, as well as the hope and freedom that come upon hearing the words, "You are forgiven."

While confession of sin involves embodied practices, so does resistance. Guided by our confessions of Christ's lordship and God's desires for justice, we resist participating in practices that belie our confession and harm others. Perhaps simply starting with refusing to participate in slanderous gossip is a good place to begin. I remained amazed in institutional contexts at the life that rumors take on, and even more amazed at how rumors and assumptions then define decisions and actions. By refusing to heed rumors and seeking more accurate descriptions of what is happening, we can begin to bring to light common concerns in order to deal with them in the light of communal commitments.

As a faculty member, I have certain privileges that come with position and a voice that can be exercised in various venues. It's okay to vote "no" publicly when decisions on which we are voting seem to work against the mission and practices to which we have committed. Even if my lone "no" vote doesn't change the outcome, it is still a practice that perhaps might be an encouragement to others to think about what we are doing and saying in our common institutional practices.

33. Ibid., 153.

34. I realize the legal and moral issues associated with confession that is made to recognized church officials—and the duty to break confidence in certain situations. The kind of confession I am exploring is a kind that happens with trusted friends, who may also need to discern when confidentiality must be broken.

Saying no is easy. Finding alternatives that give "yes" to what we should do is more difficult due to the complexities of our institutions. Mathews offers suggestions for alternative uses of power in our various institutions, particularly for those who tend to be inside institutions yet still very much marginalized.[35] She notes the ever present risk of resistance, yet as people of faith, we *must* resist practices that harm others. We can work to change our institutions in partnership with others who have our institution's well-being at heart. It's important to remember that we all benefit from how our institutions and corporations conduct business, which should guide our motivation to see change. Mathews suggests that we can also refuse to enter certain situations and institutions. Her final strategy comes from the important prophetic stream of Christian faith, in that we can commit to "work prophetically within the system."[36] This is what the prophets did in their call to fundamental reform of the legal, political, social, economic, and cultic practices of God's people, and this is what Jesus did. In order to work prophetically, Mathews reminds us of our own need for confession and self-examination. Do we want to secure power for ourselves? Is it to obtain certain privileges? Is it to secure our jobs? Confession and resistance go together in a prophetic working for the good of our institutions. While recognizing the difficulties and risks of resistance, Mathews still maintains that "it is then the task of the prophet, the person who has said 'no' to the temptation to abuse power, to create new alternatives and provide a method of hope within the system. The prophet does not just criticize but also creates within and energizes the system where possible."[37]

What a fantastic bundle of spiritually and morally formative practices: confession of God's desires, realization of our failures to embody God's desires, resistance to those practices that belie God's intentions, and struggling to embody hopeful, life-giving alternatives even in the very systems in which we live and work.

Conclusion

Confession and resistance are essential practices that form us to be hopeful. They are hopeful because they are avenues of spiritual and moral formation, and hence of change. They are practiced in our relationships with

35. Mathews, "Using Power from the Periphery," 97–102.

36. Ibid., 98.

37. Ibid., 102.

God and others. They help us gain clarity about who we are, how we fail to embody God's desires, and the ways we actually can reflect God's desires as we humbly and hopefully confess and resist. Confession shapes us to acknowledge our shortcomings and to reaffirm our loyalty to God. Confession and resistance become part of our testimony of telling the truth about ourselves, about our institutions, and about our world. Thomas Hoyt sees testimony and confessing what we hope and know to be true as a necessary form of resistance that is spoken in song, sermons, acts of charity and care, and the rituals of the church, such as the Lord's Supper and baptism. This practice of testimony as a form of resistance comes from our confession of God's liberating acts on behalf of an oppressed people.

> The practice of testimony requires a person to commit voice and body to the telling of the truth. It guards the integrity of personal and communal life, as much on the grand stage of history as in the small exchanges of home. Today, living in a world where falsehood is strong, we need to support one another as we rise to bear witness, speaking the truth about what we have seen and heard. When we do, we are also supported by another community, one that has inspired Christians since the earliest days: the "great cloud of witnesses" who have gone before us (Hebrews 12:1).[38]

We confess together that there is no other God like our God who loves justice, kindness, mercy, and humility. We confess that these, too, are our desires, yet we fail to desire them in many ways. We receive the grace, forgiveness, and freedom that God provides through confession. We struggle for new ways of saying yes to God and no to all that enslaves human lives. We do this with humility and hope, learning to trust God as we continue to orient our lives toward God's desires. May desire for God and the things that God desires remain at the center of our spiritual and moral growth as we focus on the good of others and growth in Christian virtues. May we embody and extend God's goodness to all creation.

38. Hoyt, "Testimony," 101.

Bibliography

Adams, Nicholas. "Confessing the Faith: Reasoning in Tradition." In *The Blackwell Companion to Christian Ethics*, edited by Stanley Hauerwas and Samuel Wells, 209–21. Malden, MA: Blackwell, 2004.

Albrecht, Gloria H. *The Character of Our Communities: Toward an Ethic of Liberation for the Church.* Nashville: Abingdon, 1995.

Andolsen, Barbara Hilkert. "Agape in Feminist Ethics." In *Feminist Theological Ethics: A Reader*, edited by Lois K. Daly, 146–59. Louisville: Westminster John Knox, 1994.

Baker, David W., T. Desmond Alexander, and Bruce K. Waltke. *Obadiah, Jonah, and Micah: An Introduction and Commentary.* Tyndale Old Testament Commentaries 26. Downers Grove, IL: InterVarsity, 2009.

Barclay, John M. G. *Obeying the Truth: Paul's Ethics in Galatians.* Vancouver: Regent College, 2005.

Barna Group. "Survey Finds Lots of Spiritual Dialogue but Not Much Change." Online: http://www.barna.org/transformation-articles/433-survey-finds-lots-of-spiritual-dialogue-but-not-much-change.

Bass, Dorothy C. "Keeping Sabbath." In *Practicing Our Faith: A Way of Life for a Searching People*, edited by Dorothy C. Bass, 75–88. 2nd ed. San Francisco: Jossey-Bass, 2010.

Bass, Dorothy C., editor. *Practicing Our Faith: A Way of Life for a Searching People.* 2nd ed. San Francisco: Jossey-Bass, 2010.

Bass, Dorothy C., and Craig R. Dykstra, editors. *For Life Abundant: Practical Theology, Theological Education, and Christian Ministry.* Grand Rapids: Eerdmans, 2008.

Bauckham, Richard. *God and the Crisis of Freedom: Biblical and Contemporary Perspectives.* Louisville: Westminster John Knox, 2002.

Bedford, Nancy. "Little Moves against Destructiveness: Theology and the Practice of Discernment." In *Practicing Theology: Beliefs and Practices in Christian Life*, edited by Miroslav Volf and Dorothy C. Bass, 157–81. Grand Rapids: Eerdmans, 2002.

Bellah, Robert, et al. *Habits of the Heart: Individualism and Commitment in American Life.* Berkeley: University of California Press, 1985.

Benson, Bruce Ellis, and Norman Wirzba. "Introduction." In *The Phenomenology of Prayer*, edited by Bruce Benson and Norman Wirzba, 1–12. Perspectives in Continental Philosophy 46. New York: Fordham University Press, 2005.

Billy, Dennis J., and James F. Keating. *Conscience and Prayer: The Spirit of Catholic Moral Theology.* Collegeville, MN: Liturgical, 2001.

Birch, Bruce C. *Let Justice Roll Down: The Old Testament, Ethics, and Christian Life.* Louisville: Westminster John Knox, 1991.

Bibliography

Birch, Bruce C., and Larry L. Rasmussen. *The Bible and Ethics in the Christian Life.* Minneapolis: Augsburg Fortress, 1989.

Boden, Alison L. "We Pray for the Courage to Resist." In *Resist! Christian Dissent for the Twenty-First Century*, edited by Michael G. Long, 59–61. Maryknoll, NY: Orbis, 2008.

Boff, Leonardo. *Virtues for Another Possible World.* Translated by Alexandre Guilherme. Eugene, OR: Cascade, 2011.

Bourdieu, Pierre. *An Outline of a Theory of Practice.* Translated by Richard Nice. Cambridge: Cambridge University Press, 1977.

Brown, Jeannine K., Carla M. Dahl, and Wyndy Corbin Reuschling. *Becoming Whole and Holy: An Integrative Conversation about Christian Formation.* Grand Rapids: Baker Academic, 2011.

Brown, Sally A. "Exploring the Text/Practice Interface: Acquiring the Virtue of Hermeneutical Modesty." In *Theology Today* 66:3 (2009) 274–94.

Brueggemann, Walter. *The Prophetic Imagination.* Minneapolis: Fortress, 1978.

Burridge, Richard A. *Imitating Jesus: An Inclusive Approach to New Testament Ethics.* Grand Rapids: Eerdmans, 2007.

Callahan, William. "Spirituality and Justice: An Evolving Vision of the Great Commandment." In *Contemporary Spirituality: Responding to the Divine Initiative*, edited by Francis A. Eigo, 137–61. Proceedings of the Theology Institute of Villanova University 15. Villanova: Villanova University Press, 1983.

Carroll, M. Daniel R. "'He Has Told You What Is Good': Moral Formation in Micah." In *Character Ethics and the Old Testament: Moral Dimensions of Scripture*, edited by M. Daniel Carroll R. and Jacqueline E. Lapsley, 103–18. Louisville: Westminster John Knox, 2007.

Cavanaugh, William T. *Being Consumed: Economics and Christian Desire.* Grand Rapids: Eerdmans, 2008.

Chilton, Bruce D., and J. I. H. McDonald. *Jesus and the Ethics of the Kingdom.* London: SPCK, 1987.

Clapp, Rodney. *A Peculiar People: The Church as Culture in a Post-Christian Society.* Downers Grove, IL: InterVarsity, 1996.

Connors, Russell B., Jr., and Patrick T. McCormick. *Character, Choices and Community: The Three Faces of Christian Ethics.* New York: Paulist, 1998.

Cooper, Adam G. *Life in the Flesh: An Anti-Gnostic Spiritual Philosophy.* Oxford: Oxford University Press, 2008.

Corbin Reuschling, Wyndy. "Moral Selectivity—Picking and Choosing Sex as the Barometer of Moral Decline in the Culture Wars." Unpublished paper presented at the Annual Meeting of the American Academy of Religion, Boston, MA, 1999.

———. *Reviving Evangelical Ethics: The Promises and Pitfalls of Classic Models of Morality.* Grand Rapids: Brazos, 2008.

———. "'Trust and Obey': The Danger of Obedience as Duty in Evangelical Ethics." In *The Journal of the Society of Christian Ethics* 25:2 (2005) 59–77.

Cosgrove, Bill. "Relating Spirituality and Morality." In *Doctrine and Life* 59:5 (2009) 23–28.

Crabb, Larry J. *Inside Out.* Colorado Springs: NavPress, 1980.

Crysdale, Cynthia S. W. *Embracing Travail: Retrieving the Cross Today.* New York: Continuum, 1999.

Davis, Ellen F. "Surprised by Wisdom: Preaching Proverbs." In *Interpretation* 63:3 (2009) 264–77.

Dawn, Marva J. *The Sense of the Call: A Sabbath Way of Life for Those Who Serve God, the Church, and the World*. Grand Rapids: Eerdmans, 2006.

Dayton, Donald W. *Discovering an Evangelical Heritage*. Peabody, MA: Hendrickson, 1988.

deSilva, David A. *Sacramental Life: Spiritual Formation through the Book of Common Prayer*. Downers Grove, IL: InterVarsity, 2008.

Donnelly, Doris. "Prayer: The Response of the Contemporary Christian." In *Contemporary Spirituality: Responding to the Divine Initiative*, edited by Francis A. Eigo, 63–89. Proceedings of the Theology Institute of Villanova University 15. Villanova: Villanova University Press, 1983.

Dykstra, Craig R., and Dorothy C. Bass. "A Theological Understanding of Christian Practices." In *Practicing Theology: Beliefs and Practices in Christian Life*, edited by Miroslav Volf and Dorothy C. Bass, 13–32. Grand Rapids: Eerdmans, 2002.

———. "Times of Yearning, Practices of Faith." In *Practicing Our Faith: A Way of Life for a Searching People*, edited by Dorothy C. Bass, 1–12. 2nd ed. San Francisco: Jossey-Bass, 2010.

Elliott, Matthew. "Affections." In *Dictionary of Christian Spirituality*, edited by Glen Scorgie, 248–49. Grand Rapids: Zondervan, 2011.

Elshtain, Jean Bethke. *Who Are We? Critical Reflections and Hopeful Possibilities*. Grand Rapids: Eerdmans, 2000.

Emerson, Michael, and Christian Smith. *Divided by Faith: Evangelical Religion and the Problem of Race in America*. New York: Oxford University Press, 2000.

Esler, Philip F. "Social Identity, the Virtues, and the Good Life: A New Approach to Romans 12:1—15:13." In *Biblical Theology Bulletin* 33:2 (2003) 51–63.

Everist, Norma Cook. "Gender, Power and Leadership." In *Journal of Religious Leadership* 1:2 (2002) 45–67.

Farley, Margaret. "Freedom and Desire." In *The Papers of the Henry Luce III Fellows in Theology*, edited by Matthew Zyniewicz, 57–73. Series in Theological Scholarship and Research 3. Atlanta: Scholars, 1999.

Fee, Gordon D. *Galatians*. Dorset, UK: Deo, 2007.

Felder, Cain Hope. *Troubling Biblical Waters: Race, Class, and Family*. Maryknoll, NY: Orbis, 2001.

Foster, Richard J. *Celebration of Discipline: The Path to Spiritual Growth*. 3rd ed. New York: HarperCollins, 1998.

———. *Freedom of Simplicity*. San Francisco: Harper & Row, 1981.

———. *Prayer: Finding the Heart's True Home*. New York: HarperCollins, 1992.

———. *Streams of Living Water: Celebrating the Great Traditions of Christian Faith*. San Francisco: Harper & Row, 1988.

Fretheim, Terence E. *God and World in the Old Testament: A Relational Theology of Creation*. Nashville: Abingdon, 2005.

Gaventa, Beverly R. "Galatians." In *Eerdmans Commentary on the Bible*, edited by James D. G. Dunn and John W. Rogerson, 1374–84. Grand Rapids: Eerdmans, 2003.

Geertz, Clifford. *An Interpretation of Cultures*. New York: Basic Books, 1973.

Gilligan, Carol. *In a Different Voice: Psychological Theory and Women's Development*. Cambridge: Harvard University Press, 1993.

Gonzalez, Michelle A. *Shopping: Christian Explorations of Daily Living*. Minneapolis: Fortress, 2010.

Bibliography

Greenman, Jeffrey P., and George Kalantzis, editors. *Life in the Spirit: Spiritual Formation in Theological Perspective*. Downers Grove, IL: InterVarsity, 2010.

Griffith, R. Marie. *Born Again Bodies: Flesh and Spirit in American Christianity*. Berkeley: University of California Press, 2004.

Groff, Kent Ira. "Just Praying, Acting Justly: Contemplation and Manifestation." In *Vital Christianity: Spirituality, Justice, and Christian Practice*, edited by David L. Weaver-Zercher and William Willimon, 141–53. New York: T. & T. Clark, 2005.

Groody, Daniel G. *Globalization, Spirituality, and Justice*. Maryknoll, NY: Orbis, 2009.

Gula Richard, M. *The Call to Holiness: Embracing a Fully Christian Life*. Mahwah, NJ: Paulist, 2003.

Guyon, Jeanne. *Experiencing the Depths of Jesus Christ*. Edited by Gene Edwards. Goleta, CA: Christian Books, 1975.

Haan, Roelf L. *The Economics of Honor: Biblical Reflections on Money and Property*. Translated by Bert Hielema. Grand Rapids: Eerdmans, 2009.

Harrington, Daniel J., and James F. Keenan. *Jesus and Virtue Ethics*. Lanham, MD: Rowman & Littlefield, 2002.

Hauerwas, Stanley. *A Community of Character: Toward a Constructive Christian Ethic*. Notre Dame: University of Notre Dame Press, 1981.

Hauerwas, Stanley, and Charles Pinches. *Christians Among the Virtues: Theological Conversations with Ancient and Modern Ethics*. Notre Dame: University of Notre Dame Press, 1997.

Hauerwas, Stanley, and Samuel Wells, editors. *The Blackwell Companion to Christian Ethics*. Malden, MA: Blackwell, 2004.

Hawk, L. Daniel. *Joshua in 3-D: A Commentary on Biblical Conquest and Manifest Destiny*. Eugene, OR: Cascade, 2010.

Heschel, Abraham J. *The Prophets: An Introduction*. Vol. 1. New York: Harper & Row, 1962.

———. *The Sabbath*. New York: Farrar, Straus & Giroux, 2005.

Hess, Carol Lakey. *Caretakers of Our Common House: Women's Development in Communities of Faith*. Nashville: Abingdon, 1997.

Holder, Arthur, editor. *The Blackwell Companion to Christian Spirituality*. Malden, MA: Blackwell, 2005.

Hovey, Craig. *Bearing True Witness: Truthfulness in Christian Practice*. Grand Rapids: Eerdmans, 2011.

Hoyt, Thomas. "Testimony." In *Practicing Our Faith: A Way of Life for a Searching People*, edited by Dorothy C. Bass, 89–101. San Francisco: Jossey-Bass, 2010.

Humphrey, Edith M. *Ecstasy and Intimacy: When the Holy Spirit Meets the Human Spirit*. Grand Rapids: Eerdmans, 2006.

Iosso, Christian, and Elizabeth Hinson-Hasty, editors. *Prayers for the New Social Awakening: Inspired by the New Social Creed*. Louisville: Westminster John Knox, 2008.

Jacobs, Mignon R. "Book of Micah." In *Dictionary for Theological Interpretation of the Bible*, edited by Kevin J. Vanhoozer, 512–15. Grand Rapids: Baker Academic, 2005.

Johnson, Kelly S. "Praying: Poverty." In *The Blackwell Companion to Christian Ethics*, edited by Stanley Hauerwas and Samuel Wells, 225–36. Malden, MA: Blackwell, 2004.

Kallenberg, Brad J. "Holistic Spirituality as Witness." In *Vital Christianity: Spirituality, Justice, and Christian Practice*, edited by David L. Weaver-Zercher and William Willimon, 72–87. New York: T. & T. Clark, 2005.

Kavanaugh, John F. *Following Christ in a Consumer Society*. 25th anniversary ed. Maryknoll, NY: Orbis, 2006.

King, Martin Luther, Jr. *Where Do We Go From Here: Chaos or Community?* New York: Harper & Row, 1967.

Kohlberg, Lawrence. *The Philosophy of Moral Development: Moral Stages and the Idea of Justice*. San Francisco: Harper & Row, 1981.

Kotva, Joseph. *The Christian Case for Virtue Ethics*. Washington, DC: Georgetown University Press, 1996.

Long, Michael G., editor. *Resist! Christian Dissent for the Twenty-First Century*. Maryknoll, NY: Orbis, 2008.

Long, D. Stephen, and Tripp York. "Remembering: Offering Our Gifts." In *The Blackwell Companion to Christian Ethics*, edited by Stanley Hauerwas and Samuel Wells, 332–45. Malden, MA: Blackwell, 2004.

MacIntyre, Alasdair. *After Virtue*. 2nd ed. Notre Dame: University of Notre Dame Press, 1984.

Matera, Frank J. *Galatians*. Sacra Pagina 9. Collegeville, MN: Liturgical, 1992.

Mathews, Rosita deAnn. "Using Power from the Periphery: An Alternative Model for Survival in Systems." In *A Troubling in My Soul: Womanist Perspectives on Evil and Suffering*, edited by Emilie M. Townes, 92–106. Maryknoll, NY: Orbis, 1996.

Mensch, James R. "Prayer as Kenosis." In *The Phenomenology of Prayer*, edited by Bruce Ellis Benson and Norman Wirzba, 63–74. Perspectives in Continental Philosophy 46. New York: Fordham University Press, 2005.

Meyer, Gerd. "Taking Risks for Others: Social Courage as a Public Virtue." In *On Behalf of Others: The Psychology of Care in a Global World*, edited by Sarah Scuzzarello, Catarina Kinnvall, and Kristen Renwick-Monroe, 82–105. Series in Political Psychology. Oxford: Oxford University Press, 2009.

Míguez Bonino, José. *Toward a Christian Political Ethics*. Philadelphia: Fortress, 1988.

Mott, Stephen Charles. *Biblical Ethics and Social Change*. New York: Oxford University Press, 1982.

Murphy, Nancey, Brad J. Kallenberg, and Mark Thiessen Nation, editors. *Virtues and Practices in the Christian Tradition: Christian Ethics after MacIntyre*. Harrisburg, PA: Trinity, 1997.

Noddings, Nel. *Caring: A Feminine Approach to Ethics and Moral Education*. Berkeley: University of California Press, 1984.

O'Flaherty, Edward, and Rodney Peterson with Timothy Norton, editors. *Sunday, Sabbath, and the Weekend: Managing Time in a Global Culture*. Grand Rapids: Eerdmans, 2010.

Owens, Roger L. "Sabbath-Keeping: Christian Sabbath-Keeping and the Desire for Justice." In *Vital Christianity: Spirituality, Justice, and Christian Practice*, edited by David L. Weaver-Zercher and William H. Willimon, 201–11. New York: T. & T. Clark, 2005.

Padgett, Alan B. "'Walk in the Spirit': Preaching for Spiritual Growth (Gal. 5:13–6:2)." In *Word and World* 27:3 (2007) 342–45.

Parks, Sharon Daloz. "Household Economics." In *Practicing Our Faith: A Way of Life for a Searching People*, edited by Dorothy C. Bass, 43–58. 2nd ed. San Francisco: Jossey-Bass, 2010.

Peters, Ted. *Sin: Radical Evil in Soul and Society.* Grand Rapids: Eerdmans, 1994.

Plaskow, Judith. *Sex, Sin, and Grace: Women's Experience and the Theologies of Reinhold Niebuhr and Paul Tillich.* Washington, DC: Georgetown University Press, 1980.

Pohl, Christine D. *Living into Community: Cultivating Practices that Sustain Us.* Grand Rapids: Eerdmans, 2011.

Pohl, Christine D., and Christopher Heuertz. *Friendship at the Margins: Discovering Mutuality in Service and Mission.* Downers Grove, IL: InterVarsity, 2010.

Powell, Samuel M. *A Theology of Christian Spirituality.* Nashville: Abingdon, 2005.

Pury, Cynthia L. S., and Shane J. Lopez, editors. *Psychology of Courage: Modern Research on an Ancient Virtue.* Washington, DC: American Psychological Association, 2010.

Rasmussen, Larry. *Moral Fragments and Moral Community: A Proposal for Church in Society.* Minneapolis: Fortress, 1993.

Rauschenbusch, Walter. *Prayers of the Social Awakening.* Boston: Pilgrim Press, 1910. Reprint, Eugene, OR: Wipf & Stock, 2004.

Rensberger, David. "The Love of God as the Source of Spirituality and Justice." In *Vital Christianity: Spirituality, Justice, and Christian Practice*, edited by David L. Weaver-Zercher and William Willimon, 36–46. New York: T. & T. Clark, 2005.

Roberts, Kyle A. "Eschatology and Hope." In *Dictionary of Christian Spirituality*, edited by Glen G. Scorgie, 89–94. Grand Rapids: Zondervan, 2011.

Roberts, Robert C. *Spiritual Emotions: A Psychology of Christian Virtues.* Grand Rapids: Eerdmans, 2007.

Roof, Wade Clark. *The Spiritual Marketplace: Baby Boomers and the Remaking of American Religion.* Princeton: Princeton University Press, 1999.

Rubio, Julie Hanlon. *Family Ethics: Practices for Christians.* Washington, DC: Georgetown University Press, 2010.

Saliers, Don E. "Liturgy and Ethics: Some New Beginnings." In *Liturgy and the Moral Self: Humanity at Full Stretch before God: Essays in Honor of Don E. Saliers*, edited by E. Byron Anderson and Bruce T. Morrill, 15–35. Collegeville, MN: Liturgical, 1998.

———. *The Soul in Paraphrase: Prayer and the Religious Affections.* New York: Seabury, 1980.

Santmire, H. Paul. "Healing the Protestant Mind." In *After Nature's Revolt: Eco-Justice and Theology*, edited by Dieter T. Hessel, 57–78. Minneapolis: Fortress, 1992.

Schneiders, Sandra M. "Biblical Spirituality." In *Interpretation* 56:2 (2002) 133–42.

———. "Religion vs. Spirituality: A Contemporary Conundrum." In *Spiritus* 3:2 (2003) 163–85.

Scorgie, Glen G., Simon Chan, Gordon Smith, and James Smith III, editors. *Dictionary of Christian Spirituality.* Grand Rapids: Zondervan, 2011.

Scuzzarello, Sarah, Catarina Kinnvall, and Kristen Renwick-Monroe, editors. *On Behalf of Others: The Psychology of Care in a Global World.* Series in Political Psychology. Oxford: Oxford University Press, 2009.

Selznick, Philip. *The Moral Commonwealth: Social Theory and the Promise of Community.* Berkeley: University of California Press, 1992.

Shea, John. "Jesus' Response to God as Abba: Prayer and Service." In *Contemporary Spirituality: Responding to the Divine Initiative*, edited by Francis A. Eigo, 33–62. Proceedings of the Theology Institute of Villanova University 15. Villanova: Villanova University Press, 1983.

Sheldrake, Philip. "Desire." In *The New Westminster Dictionary of Christian Spirituality*, edited by Philip Sheldrake, 231–33. Louisville: Westminster John Knox, 2005.

Shults, F. LeRon, and Steven J. Sandage. *Transforming Spirituality: Integrating Theology and Psychology*. Grand Rapids: Baker Academic, 2006.

Smith, Gordon T. "Penitence." In *Dictionary of Christian Spirituality*, edited by Glen G. Scorgie, 661–63. Grand Rapids: Zondervan, 2011.

Smith, James K. A. *Desiring the Kingdom: Worship, Worldview, and Cultural Formation*. Grand Rapids: Baker Academic, 2009.

Snyder, Howard. *The Community of the King*. 2nd ed. Downers Grove, IL: InterVarsity, 2004.

Spohn, William B. *Go and Do Likewise: Jesus and Ethics*. New York: Continuum, 2006.

———. *What Are They Saying about Scripture and Ethics?* Rev. ed. Mahwah, NJ: Paulist, 1995.

Stassen, Glen H., and David P. Gushee. *Kingdom Ethics: Following Jesus in Contemporary Context*. Downers Grove, IL: InterVarsity, 2003.

Strum, Douglas. "Resisting Individualism, Advocating Solidarity." In *Resist! Christian Dissent for the Twenty-First Century*, edited by Michael G. Long, 137–58. Maryknoll, NY: Orbis, 2008.

Sweeney, Marvin A. *The Twelve Prophets*. Vol. 2, *Micah, Nahum, Habakkuk, Zephaniah, Haggai, Zechariah, Malachi*. Collegeville, MN: Liturgical, 2000.

Tanner, Kathryn. "Theological Reflection and Christian Practices." In *Practicing Theology: Beliefs and Practices in Christian Life*, edited by Miroslav Volf and Dorothy C. Bass, 228–42. Grand Rapids: Eerdmans, 2002.

Townes, Emilie M. "Living in the New Jerusalem." In *A Troubling in My Soul: Womanist Perspectives on Evil and Suffering*, edited by Emilie M. Townes, 78–91. Maryknoll, NY: Orbis, 1993.

Tutu, Desmond. *No Future Without Forgiveness*. New York: Doubleday, 1999.

Ukwuegbu, Bernard O. "Paraenesis, Identity-Defining Norms, or Both? Galatians 5:13—6:10 in the Light of Social Identity Theory." In *The Catholic Biblical Quarterly* 70 (2008) 538–59.

Ven, J. A. van der. *Formation of the Moral Self*. Grand Rapids: Eerdmans, 1998.

Verhey, Allen. *Remembering Jesus: Christian Community, Scripture, and the Moral Life*. Grand Rapids: Eerdmans, 2002.

Volf, Miroslav. *The End of Memory: Remembering Rightly in a Violent World*. Grand Rapids: Eerdmans, 2006.

Volf, Miroslav, and Dorothy C. Bass, editors. *Practicing Theology: Beliefs and Practices in Christian Life*. Grand Rapids: Eerdmans, 2002.

Washington, James Melvin, editor. *Conversations with God: Two Centuries of Prayers by African Americans*. New York: HarperCollins, 1994.

Weaver-Zercher, David L., and William H. Willimon, editors. *Vital Christianity: Spirituality, Justice, and Christian Practice*. New York: T. & T. Clark, 2005.

Weinfeld, Moshe. *Social Justice in Ancient Israel and in the Ancient Near East*. Jerusalem: Magnes Press/The Hebrew University, 1995.

Welch, Sharon. *A Feminist Ethic of Risk*. Minneapolis: Fortress, 1990.

Wirzba, Norman. *Living the Sabbath: Discovering the Rhythms of Rest and Delight*. Grand Rapids: Brazos, 2006.

Witvliet, Charlotte vanOyen, Nova G. Hinman, Timothy Brandt, and Julie J. Exline. "Responding to Our Own Transgressions: An Experimental Writing Study of Repentance, Offense Rumination, Self-Justification, and Distraction." In *Journal of Psychology and Christianity* 31:3 (2011) 223–37.

Bibliography

Wolterstorff, Nicholas. *Hearing the Call: Liturgy, Justice, Church, and World: Essays.* Edited by Mark R. Gornik and Gregory Thompson. Grand Rapids: Eerdmans, 2011.

———. *Justice: Rights and Wrongs.* Princeton: Princeton University Press, 2008.

Wright, Christopher, J. H. "The Earth Is the Lord's: Biblical Foundations for Global Ecological Ethics and Mission." In *Keeping God's Earth: The Global Environment in Biblical Perspective,* edited by Noah J. Toly and Daniel I. Block, 216–42. Downers Grove, IL: InterVarsity, 2010.

———. *Old Testament Ethics for the People of God.* Downers Grove, IL: InterVarsity, 2004.

Wuthnow, Robert. *After Heaven: Spirituality in America since the 1950s.* Berkeley: University of California Press, 1998.

Yoder, John Howard. *The Politics of Jesus.* 2nd ed. Grand Rapids: Eerdmans, 1994.

Young, Iris Marion. *Justice and the Politics of Difference.* Princeton: Princeton University Press, 1990.

Zuliani, Liz. "A Dozen Alarming Consumer Debt Statistics." *Economy Watch,* 21 May 2011. Online: http://www.economywatch.com/economy-business-and-finance-news/a-dozen-alarming-consumer-debt-statistics.21-05.html.

Subject Index

Subject Index

global contexts/globalization, 40, 72, 81, 88, 96, 100

God, Trinitarian/Triune, xv, 6, 17, 24, 41, 43, 103, 106

good/goodness, 24, 26, 32, 37–38, 47, 61, 110, 116, 121

  good of others, 13, 14, 21–22, 37–38, 45, 69, 70, 90–91, 112, 121

gratitude, 8, 64, 81, 91, 93–95, 98

H

habits, 26, 28, 40–41, 50, 53, 55, 59, 63, 81, 88–89, 96

Holy Spirit (the), xv, 6, 8, 14, 11, 17, 20, 21–22, 28, 40, 42, 47, 50, 103, 105, 117

  fruit of, 8, 11, 13, 15, 16–19, 20, 21, 22, 92

  walking in the Spirit, 15, 16, 19–20

hope, 6, 8, 15, 20, 31–32, 41, 65, 67, 103, 105, 74, 114–17, 119, 120–21

human beings, 2, 13, 28, 51, 59, 83, 88, 113

human flourishing, 36, 43, 67, 76, 82

humanity, 6, 38, 39, 84, 113, 115

humility, 33–34, 38, 41, 44, 90, 103, 109, 114–17, 121

I

individualism, 2, 102, 105

  individualistic spirituality, 20, 55

institutions, 2, 4, 5, 33, 43, 66–67, 73–74, 79, 107, 108, 110, 119–20

interdependence, 42, 53, 75, 84

J

Jesus Christ, xii, xvi, xv, 3, 6, 8, 12, 13, 14, 17, 20, 25, 28, 40, 50, 54, 56–57, 62, 65, 75–76, 86, 98, 103, 104, 107–9, 114–15, 117–18

justice, xiii– xv, 6, 8, 9, 28, 29–37, 38–40, 42, 44, 45, 54–55, 60, 63, 65, 67, 70–72, 75, 78, 79,

86–87, 90, 91–92, 99, 106–8, 109, 110–11, 112

K

kingdom of God, xiii, 13, 14, 50, 85–87

L

Lord's Supper, 58–59, 112

  Eucharist, 93–94

love(s), xiii, xv, 5–7, 13, 14–15, 17, 18, 19, 26–27, 34, 36–37, 51, 53, 61, 65, 82–83, 84, 93, 104–6, 107, 109, 118, 121

  loving kindness, 32, 39

  of God, 13, 36, 51, 59, 61

  of neighbor, 13, 44, 51, 70, 111

M

mercy, xiii, 30, 31, 34, 36, 42, 44–45, 60, 65, 69, 71, 90, 98, 105, 107, 109

Micah (book of), 30–32

money, 82, 84, 90–91, 97–9

morality, xvii–xviii, 2, 7, 24–25, 37, 41–42, 47–48

moral formation, xvi–xvii, 22, 26, 27, 29, 37–38, 43, 47–48, 51, 53, 54, 57, 61, 63, 69, 118

moral vision, 26–28, 49, 115

O

obedience, 11, 25, 27–28, 32

P

passion(s), 8, 50, 69, 106–7, 109

piety, xii, 18, 29–30, 36, 42, 48

power, 2, 4, 30–31, 32, 44, 52, 60, 70, 73, 74, 77, 78, 83, 101, 102, 108, 113, 114, 115, 119, 120

practices, xviii–xx, 1, 2, 5, 6–7, 10, 12, 19, 21, 23, 30, 35–36, 41, 48, 49–53, 54–61 74, 80, 84–85, 87, 93, 96

  definition of, xviii–xix, 49, 51

  ethical, xvi, xvii–xviii, 11, 48, 50, 53, 55

DATE DUE
